It Happened In Series

IT HAPPENED IN
FLORIDA

E. Lynne Wright

TWODOT®

GUILFORD, CONNECTICUT
HELENA, MONTANA
AN IMPRINT OF THE GLOBE PEQUOT PRESS

A · TWODOT® · BOOK

Cover illustration © 2003 by Lisa Harvey, Helena, Montana

The publisher gratefully acknowledges the assistance of Robert A. Taylor, Ph.D., Associate Professor of History, Florida Institute of Technology.

Library of Congress Cataloging-in-Publication Data
Wright, E. Lynne, 1931–
   It happened in Florida/E. Lynne Wright.—1st ed.
      p. cm.—(It happened in series)
   Includes bibliographical references (p.) and index.
   ISBN 0-7627-1054-3
     1. Florida—History—Anecdotes. I. Title. II. Series.
F311.6.W75 2002
975.9—dc21

2002072217

Manufactured in the United States of America
First Edition/Second Printing

Contents

Preface

Like so many other people, I came to Florida from somewhere else, drawn here by the chance to escape northern winters, not anticipating anything other than sunny days, good boating, and lots of navel oranges. Florida history was the last thing on my mind, but I kept bumping into some of the same names over and over. Henry Flagler, for one. His name seemed to pop up everywhere. There was Flagler Beach, Flagler County, the railroad he built, and his hotels that rivaled the Taj Mahal. His private life, I discovered, was even more interesting.

What was so special about someone named Osceola? He was a Native American, obviously, but why did I run into his name every time I turned a corner?

Make a trip to the Everglades and inevitably the name Marjory Stoneman Douglas will come up. But she had so much more to her credit than simply being a champion of the Everglades (as if that weren't enough). What a woman!

Slowly, I became hooked. So many fascinating things have happened in Florida. And why not? European history got started on this continent in 1513 in Florida, not on that big rock in Massachusetts in 1620. By that time, St. Augustine already had shops, a church, and a hospital. The Pilgrims were the new kids on the block.

The same climate and sunny days that brought me to Florida have brought other folks, too, from New York, Ontario, Havana, Russia—you name it—some for vacations, others as part-time "snowbirds." Some lucky ones like me have made Florida their year-round home. There's good and bad in that. Being home to so many people from somewhere else keeps things interesting in the Sunshine State, but it can lead to divided allegiances. Their bodies tan in this sunny paradise, but their hearts and their families reside somewhere else.

This might have something to do with the well-established Florida tradition: "Take the money and run." Everyone, it seems, wants to take something from Florida. What's taken these days might be happy memories and a pair of "mouse ears," but in the past it included pinewood forests, egret feathers, Seminole tribal lands, turtle eggs, and alligator skins. As fast as the bolts of lightning that slash our summer skies, the word went out. Florida has been in the midst of a development boom ever since—to the benefit of our economy but to the detriment of our environment.

Generally speaking, people don't concern themselves much with Florida history. Instead they concentrate mainly on what has happened lately in the state: Elian and his feuding family, shark attacks, bungled elections, and Middle Eastern fanatics taking flying lessons.

Reading Florida history can be comforting. It reminds us that people in the past survived the same things we're facing today. Current ads for in-home shelters to ensure safety from bio-terrorists are echoes of backyard bomb shelters hastily built during the Cuban missile crisis. Although they didn't manage to inflict much damage, Nazi saboteurs invaded our shores in 1942, long before the foreign terrorists of 2001. The election of 1876 was no more satisfying to half the nation than the election in 2000, but we survived them both. We made it before; we'll do it again.

Floridians will continue putting out the welcome mat, hoping snowbirds, transplants, and tourists, too, will come for the sunshine but also take time to check into the fascinating history of this lovely peninsula. As well as being comforting, finding out what happened in Florida can be fun—a day at the beach, you might say.

Acknowledgments

I owe so much to so many who helped me with the research of this book. I want to first thank the super-resourceful, extra-efficient reference librarians at the Indian River County Main Library in Vero Beach. Their help in locating sources was invaluable. Special thanks to Peg Wilson. I also thank the University of Florida College of Medicine for sharing Dr. Cade's oral history interview. Thanks to the Indian River County Audubon Society for making their files on Marjorie Carr available to me. Barbara Ware, Archivist and Librarian assisted me at the beautiful Tampa Bay History Center, then continued to supply me with information by e-mail. Although grieving the loss of her husband, Betty Skelton Frankman graciously took time to furnish me with a packet of material for which I am most grateful. Thanks to Dennis Wilhelm, Archivist at Miami's Arquitectonica for the excellent leads he offered for Barbara Capitman's story. I am indebted to the archivists at the Florida State Archives in Tallahassee for their assistance with the Roxcy Bolton files. Nicole Palovich was so cordial and informative at Give Kids the World, it was hard to leave the Village. I'm grateful to the Sanford L. Ziff Jewish Museum for generously sharing their files on Ruby Diamond. I thank Kevin Quirk, General Manager of the Bahia Mar Resort, who filled me in on slip F-18 and who stands guard over Travis McGee's bottle of Plymouth Gin. How can I possibly thank my editor, Charlene Patterson? She's just the greatest. Finally, I thank my husband and family, as fine a bunch of cheerleaders as can be found anywhere.

Ponce de León's Reception in the New World

·1513·

From the beginning immigrants have sometimes received a less-than-warm welcome in the New World. Juan Ponce de León was no exception. In fact, the man who is credited with discovering Florida had such an ignominious debut in America, he spent very little actual time on our soil before fleeing for his life.

Florida's recorded history began with Ponce, a Spanish nobleman who, like other explorers of his day, was unquestionably motivated by a quest for power, riches, and natives to enslave.

The myth of the Fountain of Youth, so firmly attached to Ponce's name, probably started with Indians repeating tales about healing waters told to them by other European explorers. The legend of such a fountain or spring existed in many parts of the world and could be traced to the fabled "water of life" in the Garden of Eden, supposedly located in the Far East. Early Spanish explorers thought America was the Far East, possibly convincing some that the fountain must be somewhere in the New World. Bearing in mind that neither Spaniards nor Indians were bilingual and Spanish explorers needed to periodically replenish their drinking water, it seems logical that requests for "fresh" or "sweet" water could be interpreted as rejuvenating water from a spring or fountain.

The only existing source containing firsthand details of Ponce's journey is a monumental ten-volume work published about 1610. It contains no mention of a Fountain of Youth. The lures of finding gold and conquering new territories were the usual reasons for men to explore strange lands, and there is little reason to doubt these reasons were uppermost in Ponce de León's mind as well.

Ponce had sailed with Christopher Columbus's second voyage to the New World in 1493, when Puerto Rico was discovered. At that time Ponce remained on the island of Hispaniola to establish a settlement and enslave natives to mine the gold deposits he expected to find. The Spanish king rewarded him with the governorship of eastern Hispaniola (now the Dominican Republic), then the governorship of Puerto Rico. Accordingly, Ponce's wealth increased.

However, during the palace intrigue following Columbus's death, his son, Diego Columbus, claimed all his father's possessions, along with the right to install his own people as governors. Being unceremoniously ousted from his job must have been the irritant that helped energize Ponce to pursue his own discoveries and add to his wealth and prestige.

In 1513 he set out from Puerto Rico with three ships, heading north until he reached what he thought was an island, probably near what is now the city of Melbourne, Florida. Over the years St. Augustine has claimed to be the spot where the Spaniards landed, dispensing water from its springs to eager tourists, but studies of Ponce's navigation log using modern instruments render this unlikely. Additionally, one can't help but notice that there are no records of tourists enjoying incredibly long life spans after quenching their thirst in St. Augustine.

Since it was the Easter season, *Pascua florida,* and the land "had a very beautiful view of many and cool woodlands," Ponce named it *La Florida,* "Land of Flowers." Under the patent granted him by King Ferdinand, Ponce claimed his discovery for Spain. Heading south, he made a second discovery, although at the time he did not recognize it for what it was.

As Ponce's three vessels followed the coast, it became increasingly difficult to make forward progress despite strong winds in their favor. Gradually, the current became stronger than the wind, causing the ships to regress rather than sail forward. The two caravels nearest land dropped anchor, but the smaller brigantine in deeper waters was unable to anchor. Carried out to sea, it disappeared from sight.

The Spaniards had discovered a "river" 50 to 300 miles wide in the ocean. Ponce de León's pilot, realizing its significance, made notes for charting a route for ships to be carried on their voyages home, a great boon to Spanish exploration. Today, we call this "river" the Gulf Stream. Even now, large tankers traveling north ride the Gulf Stream to save valuable time.

While his ship lay at anchor awaiting the return of the brigantine, several Indians waved to Ponce from shore. Thinking he had found some likely prospects to mine the riches he expected to find on his "island," Ponce waved back as he began rowing ashore with some men. A sudden flurry of bone-tipped arrows and spears rained down, convincing the Spaniards to await the return of the brigantine from a safer distance.

As they replenished firewood and water near what was later called Jupiter Inlet, they might well have wondered if their ungracious welcome was due to messages carried to the Indians by escaped Caribbean slaves, victims of Ponce de León's suppression of Puerto Rican natives.

After reuniting with their missing ship, Ponce and his men sailed on to the last of the keys, where they feasted on turtles, appropriately naming the islands the Tortugas. Replenishing wood and water again, they sailed north as far as Sanibel Island, where they careened one ship for repairs. As they worked, an Indian shouted in Spanish from a distance, saying his chief would like to trade much gold with them. The wary Ponce only waved back in response, but shortly afterward, Indians in canoes were grabbing the anchor line, attempting to drag Ponce's ship to shore while others began an assault. The Spaniards fought them off and, having had their fill of unfriendly Indians, sailed back to the safety of Puerto Rico.

In his seven-month journey, Ponce had been greeted by hostile natives, was unable to establish a permanent settlement, and, to his great disappointment, had no fabulous wealth to show for his trouble.

Unaware that he had actually discovered the tip of a new continent, he remained in Puerto Rico, accruing wealth to finance more expeditions. Reports of successful discoveries by other explorers tormented him, especially tales of the vast riches Hernando Cortés sent to Spain from his conquest of Mexico.

In 1521 Ponce decided to try again. Armed with documents naming him governor of Florida and intending to establish a colony where he would get his share of the fabulous wealth of the New World, he set out with soldiers, farmers, priests, supplies, cows, and other animals. He anchored off Estero Bay, near Fort Myers Beach, close to where he had been eight years previously.

Whether or not the same Indians recognized him and his party, their greeting was much the same—a fierce attack. An arrow pierced Ponce's armor, wounding him seriously. His men carried him to the ship and hastily departed the Land of Flowers, setting sail for Cuba, where Ponce died of his wounds. His body was returned to Puerto Rico and buried.

Ponce de León died unaware of the true significance of the "island" he claimed for Spain, or the importance of the great "river" he discovered in the ocean, or even that the Andalusia cattle he took along on the 1521 voyage would be the forbears of modern Florida's thriving cattle industry. He barely set foot on his "island" and never glimpsed gold, but he became more famous in ensuing English history books than he did among his Spanish contemporaries.

Florida's first governor would surely be pleased that part of his discovery would one day be known as the Gold Coast, some of the most highly valued property in the richest nation in the world.

Osceola Betrayed
· 1838 ·

In 1786 Thomas Jefferson loftily proclaimed, "It may be regarded as certain that not a foot of land will ever be taken from the Indians without their consent."

After that, things went downhill.

A treaty signed in 1823, supposedly effective for twenty years and no bargain for Florida's Seminoles to begin with, was violated in 1830 with President Andrew Jackson's signing of the Indian Removal Bill. Then the newest government Indian agent, Wiley Thompson, asked the Seminoles to sign yet another treaty, which would move them to undesirable lands in the West amid other Indian tribes who were their enemies. In response, a charismatic young Seminole named Osceola whipped out his knife, stabbed the treaty on the council table, and snarled, "This is the only treaty I will ever make with the whites!"

The legend of Osceola had begun.

His name, *Asi Yahola,* corrupted by whites into Osceola, would become one of the most famous of all Indian names. Born about 1803, he denied stories of being a half-breed, announcing emphatically, "No foreign blood runs in my veins. I am a pure-blood. . . ." His mother was Creek, and since Creek and Seminole tribal structure was matrilineal, he was a member of his mother's clan, justified in claiming descent and inheritance from her.

Although he was not a chief by heredity and his time of influence was brief, he not only led his own people but was destined to become the idol of many whites.

After the treaty-stabbing incident, Osceola seldom missed an opportunity to show contempt for white men's treaties. He shot agent Thompson in 1835, causing a further rift in American-Seminole relations and sparking the Second Seminole War. Thompson grew to hate Osceola so much that during one acrimonious session in his office, the agent had him jailed with his wrists bound tightly enough that scars formed. Osceola, nearly insane with anger, raged for hours, then plotted revenge. Released six days later, still seething inwardly, he pretended to be remorseful. His performance must have been convincing because the grateful Thompson gifted him with a custom-made rifle—a major error on his part, as it turned out.

Some time later, when Thompson and a companion were out for a stroll, Osceola, brandishing his new rifle, stepped from behind some trees. After killing both men, Osceola scalped Thompson and, as payback, cut his scalp into pieces, giving each Indian in his group a souvenir.

Newspapers reported Osceola's escapades, including his badgering of government troops and outsmarting of several generals. He watched his enemies from a distance, marveling at their clumsy, noisy maneuverings, so unlike the Indians' silent movements through the forests.

But both Seminoles and whites tired as the feud dragged on. Food, energy, and ammunition were running low and any trust they ever had in each other had run out.

Finally, Osceola agreed to meet for peace talks with the latest white commander, General Thomas S. Jesup, under a flag of truce. Like all Seminoles, Osceola regarded the white flag as almost sacred. But once inside the camp, his party was surrounded, and he was knocked on the head, bound, and thrown into a cell.

As word of the betrayal spread, the entire nation and even other nations were outraged and disgusted. Congress investigated Jesup, ending up evenly divided for and against him. His name became synonymous with treachery and he spent much of the rest of his life defending his actions.

Osceola had been suffering from intermittent fevers, now thought to have been malaria. He was tired, ill, and defeated. His two wives and one child were permitted to join him in prison at Fort Marion in St. Augustine, the oldest fort in the United States. The man who had lived easily in a vast forest and bathed in clean rivers spent the next five weeks in the overcrowded fort, experiencing a recurrence of his illness exacerbated by poor hygiene and an infestation of fleas. (Recently, scientists examined strands of Osceola's hair that were among artifacts passed to descendants of his attending physicians. Tests indicated that Osceola suffered from head lice which, untreated, could also cause fevers and chills.)

As more Indians were captured, the prison became even more crowded and sanitation deteriorated. A measles outbreak followed by a prison escape contributed to the decision to move the prisoners to a safer site. Fort Moultrie in Charleston, South Carolina, was chosen. The incarcerated Indians would be removed from their homeland after all.

During his imprisonment, Osceola was attended by the Fort Marion physician, Dr. Frederick Weedon, a colonel in Andrew Jackson's army who had settled in St. Augustine. Osceola had developed acute tonsillitis, a serious condition in those times. Trust between doctor and patient grew to the point that, when the Indians found out they were to be moved, Osceola asked that Weedon accompany them.

Though something of a celebrity and well-treated by his captors, Osceola's life ebbed. Dr. Weedon visited him every few hours and consulted with his friend, Dr. Benjamin Strobel, Professor of Anatomy in Charleston. Both physicians did everything they could, but Seminole medicine men who were present prevented several measures the doctors felt would benefit the patient. Dr. Weedon recorded in his diary that Osceola asked "that his Bones Should be permitted to remain in peace and that I should take them To Florida & place them where I Knew they would not be disturbed."

Early on January 30, 1838, with Weedon present, Osceola asked for his best clothes. He dressed, painted half of his face, hands, and knife handle with red paint—an oath of war—smilingly shook hands all around with Indians and whites alike, laid back grasping his scalping knife, crossed his hands, and died.

Even then, the indignities did not stop. Dr. Weedon, Osceola's best white friend, during a moment alone with the corpse, beheaded the body.

Several theories attempt to explain this bizarre behavior, but none explains it any better than the doctor's great-granddaughter who said, "Dr. Weedon was an unusual man. . . ." While the warrior's body was buried at Fort Moultrie, in Charleston, South Carolina, Dr. Weedon embalmed the head and took it with him when he returned to St. Augustine, keeping it in his home where he also had his office. His great-granddaughter related that when one of his sons misbehaved, the doctor would hang the embalmed head from the boy's bedpost to teach him a lesson. An unusual man indeed.

Eventually, Weedon gave the head to his son-in-law, a Dr. Whitehurst, who, in turn, sent it to his former professor, Dr. Valentine Mott, a New York City surgeon. White historians think the head was destroyed in a fire at the medical college where Dr. Mott kept specimens. However, Seminoles, citing Mott's statement that he was keeping the head at his home, believe it still exists.

Since the 1930s, Florida and South Carolina have argued intermittently about who should have Osceola's grave. Charleston believes it would become "just another tourist attraction" in Florida. Florida accuses Charleston of "gross neglect" of the grave, citing a 1966 incident when a park guard discovered that someone had been digging at the gravesite. Immediately after the discovery, local police were joined by the FBI and news reporters. By that time Fort Moultrie National Monument was under the authority of the National Park Service, which began an archeological investigation. The investigation disclosed a headless skeleton still in the grave identified as belonging to Osceola.

Although few outside their families and some historians remember Jesup, Thompson, or Weedon, in the United States there are three counties, two townships, twenty towns, one borough, one state park, two lakes, a national forest, and a dormitory hall at Florida State University that bear the name of the Seminole warrior Osceola.

Despite his deathbed request, Osceola's bones are still not in their Florida home.

Dr. Gorrie Makes Ice
· 1842 ·

During the summer of 1841, over one hundred people died in Apalachicola when the Gulf port town, one of Florida's most important seaports, reeled under the annual recurrence of yellow fever and malaria. One local physician, Dr. John Gorrie, obsessed with learning to control the fevers, worked devotedly, caring for patients in two regional hospitals. The recurrence of the illnesses during months of soaring heat and humidity led him to deduce that the possible cause might be airborne miasmas from decomposing vegetation.

Dr. Gorrie had been the postmaster, city council chairman, treasurer, and mayor while he maintained interests in the Mansion House Hotel, two banks, and the Apalachicola Land Company. He also founded Trinity Church in Apalachicola in the days before he became obsessed with the all-consuming goal of helping people suffering from the fevers. Capitalizing on the goodwill he had earned among his fellow citizens, he constantly harangued them to drain swamps and use mosquito nets to filter from the air the poisons he believed were causing the sicknesses. Whenever he could spare a moment, he shut himself in the laboratory attached to his house, searching for a means to dry and cool the air in his patients' rooms in hopes of controlling their fevers.

Success finally arrived on a June afternoon in 1842. Normally shy and reserved, the doctor recognized that what he had accomplished would have far-reaching effects and, eager to share the news, he rushed to find his friend, Dr. Alvan Chapman, who was mixing prescriptions in his dispensary. Dr. Chapman was one of the few who knew about Gorrie's search for a way of reducing patients' temperatures.

"Well," Dr. Chapman said, "have you found a way to freeze your patients?"

"No, but I've made ice!" was Dr. Gorrie's astounding announcement.

During experiments with cooling air, Gorrie had accidentally produced small blocks of "artificial" ice. Although benefiting patients was always his primary concern, he realized there could be other as-yet undreamed-of possibilities in the making of ice. Someday, he predicted, foods could be frozen solid to preserve them, an improvement over salting, pickling, and drying, which were then the only means of food preservation.

Chapman, a botanist, was excited for his friend. He later assisted him with a demonstration at the Mansion House Hotel, organized by an M. Rosan, a French cotton buyer who lived in Apalachicola during the shipping season.

Since about 1805, New England ship owners had chopped ice from lakes and rivers in the region, loaded it into insulated ships and sold it to Southern cities. The larger cities built huge, insulated vaults to store the blocks of ice. Unfortunately, after stops in Savannah and Charleston, the ships were sometimes empty by the time they reached the docks in Apalachicola. When ships failed to arrive at all, as frequently happened, mint juleps were served warm.

On this occasion, even though no ice ship had been in port for some time, M. Rosan dazzled his guests with chilled champagne before moving the entire party to Gorrie's laboratory, where the doctor demonstrated his ice-making machine.

The machine consisted of two compressor pumps—one to compress air, the other to expand it—both run by steam, with a storage chamber in between to feed cool air through pipes into patients' rooms. When the cool air passed around a container of water, ice formed.

Properly impressed, the party then proceeded to a room used for fever patients, where, on that sweltering summer evening, the air was delightfully dry, cool, and comfortable. A basin of ice had been suspended from the ceiling with a pipe extending from the basin through a hole in the ceiling to the chimney, allowing air to enter the room. With the doors and windows closed and another pipe at floor level, air entered the room at the ceiling, was cooled by the ice in the basin, and was drawn to the floor where it was discharged to the outside.

The guests were astounded and the news circulated quickly, though not to everyone's delight. "If the Lord intended ice in Florida, He would have put it there," was one pious man's objection.

Accumulating wealth had never been Dr. Gorrie's ambition; the possibility of eliminating illness and death was always uppermost in his mind. However, Gorrie needed to begin a search for financial backers since his own finances and those of his wife had been exhausted by his research and attempts to launch the manufacture of his invention. The one backer who came forward died suddenly, and by some strange legal twist, Gorrie was declared legally responsible for the backer's debts as well as his own.

His application for a patent was approved in 1851, but in the meantime, as a search for funding went on, a crusade of disparagement began. New England ship owners, aware that Dr. Gorrie's ice machine could spell disaster for their lucrative ice trade, enlisted Northern newspapers in a campaign of ridicule. "How could you trust a man who said he made ice in Florida in the summer?" one asked. "If a man could produce this miracle, why couldn't he get financing?" said another.

The scheme worked. No other backer came forth. Dr. Gorrie, desiring only the alleviation of human suffering as a reward for his work, was discouraged and heartbroken at the organized derision. He retired to his home, forgotten by all but his family and his ever-faithful friend, Dr. Chapman, who made the truth known about him wherever and whenever he could.

Ironically, Dr. Gorrie himself was stricken by a fever when he was just fifty-two years old, and he died on June 29, 1853.

Five years later, a Parisian friend of M. Rosan's, Ferdinand Carré, amid reports that he had profited considerably from hints leaked to him about Dr. Gorrie's work, claimed to be the inventor of the first ice-making machine. The manufacture of ice soon became commonplace.

Chapman continued to keep his friend's name alive until 1897, when ice merchant Samuel Whitehead enlisted fellow members of the Southern Ice Exchange to fund a memorial for Dr. Gorrie. Whitehead proposed that each merchant donate the proceeds from the sale of one ton of ice for a monument to honor the man to whom they owed so much. The grateful members agreed, and the memorial in front of Trinity Church in Apalachicola was dedicated in 1900.

Befitting one of the nineteenth century's great inventors, the original model of Dr. Gorrie's machine is on exhibit in the Smithsonian Institution. In 1914, the doctor's great-granddaughter, Florida senators, Samuel Whitehead, and members of the Southern Ice Exchange were present at the unveiling of a marble likeness of the great inventor and humanitarian in the National Statuary Hall in the Capitol in Washington, D.C.

Barefoot Mailmen
· 1887 ·

In the late nineteenth century, long before the U.S. Post Office faced anthrax spores or employees "going postal," south Florida mail carriers dealt with wild animals, mail routes that took a week to complete, and a workplace that was literally a jungle.

The distance between Miami and Palm Beach is 68 miles, but in the mid-1800s, a letter sent between those cities would be transported by boat to Key West, Cuba, New York, and Jacksonville before arriving at its destination, some 3,000 miles and six to eight weeks later. As the population increased, people demanded more dependable mail delivery, resulting in a service so unique that the carriers became legends. Officially, it was called a "star route," a mail delivery route contracted to a private carrier. But it became better known as the route of the barefoot mailmen—the stuff of postcards, billboards, a novel, a motion picture, and a gift boutique in a Palm Beach mall.

At the time, there were no roads, no railroads, not even a path between Miami and Palm Beach. So desolate was the area that in 1875 the U.S. Life Saving Service began building five Houses of Refuge at intervals along the coast for shipwrecked sailors who otherwise had little chance of survival, unless they could, against all odds, signal a passing steamer. Short of hacking through the jungle with a machete, the beach was the only way across the land. Thus the mail carriers took to the sand.

Barefoot mailmen, eleven in all, were necessarily young, strong, brave, and healthy. They had to be, to cover 138 miles round-trip in six days, rest one day, then start all over again the following day—all in the searing Florida sun, confronting torrential rains or hurricanes, facing mosquitoes and wild animals. The salary for walking 8,000 miles a year was $600 annually, but less if men were late or absent, which happened just two times.

The first incident of tardiness occurred in 1886, when the few settlers along the route awakened to find their beach covered with hundreds of casks of wine—Spanish claret, according to the labels. It was said that in one area, casks were so close together along the beach that one could have walked a mile without stepping in sand. Over 50 miles of beach, from Biscayne Bay to the Indian River, were strewn with casks of claret, interspersed with fifteen-gallon kegs of Malaga and Double Superior, all bearing Spanish labels. Strangely, no other wreckage ever appeared, nor did settlers hear of any wreck along the coast. Within a week, all the casks disappeared, some washed out to sea, others confiscated by settlers in what became known as the "Great Wine Wreck." Reasons for the late mail delivery that week were suspect, but the settlers were blissfully unconcerned.

The barefoot mailmen's usual routine was as follows:

Monday: Pick up mail in Palm Beach. Sail down Lake Worth to Boyton Inlet. Walk 5 miles across Boyton Beach. Rest the first night at Orange Grove House of Refuge in Delray Beach.

Tuesday: Walk 7 miles to Hillsborough Inlet. Cross the inlet in a small government boat kept hidden in the bushes for that purpose. Walk 18 miles to Fort Lauderdale and spend the second night at the New River House of Refuge.

Wednesday: Row 4 miles down New River to the inlet. Walk 10 miles to the top of Biscayne Bay. Sail if the wind was favorable; row if it was not. Reach Miami Wednesday night.

Thursday: Begin return trip in the morning.

The men would return to Palm Beach late Saturday night, having traveled approximately 80 miles on foot and 56 by boat. They would rest on Sunday and start over again on Monday morning. To prevent fatigue, the mailmen developed a peculiar, barefoot walk on the hard-packed, slanting sand at the water's edge. Heading south, the right foot moved a bit quicker than the left. Heading north, the left moved more quickly.

They tied their shoes together and slung them over their shoulders along with their mail sack and a haversack. The U.S. Post Office permitted barefoot mailmen to carry lightweight canvas mail sacks rather than the standard cowhide ones used in the rest of the country. The haversack held hard biscuits, salt pork, coffee, a small frying pan, a tin cup, and matches. The mailmen fortified their scanty diet with fish from the ocean, oysters found near roots in the water, and wild oranges and bananas. Occasional turtle eggs were a special treat, and sea grape leaves made fine dishes. Caves supplied shelter from sudden storms and drinking water was collected in barrels scattered along the way.

While the barefoot mailmen sometimes experienced harrowing encounters with alligators, panthers, poisonous snakes, wild boars, and bears, not to mention swarms of mosquitoes and sand flies, they also were the exclusive audience for exuberant dolphins and fish jumping from the water, sandpipers playing at the water's edge, the amazing straight-down dives of pelicans, and blue herons meditating. They discovered treasure troves of sand dollars and other perfect shells seemingly reserved for them alone.

The fall of 1887 was an unusually stormy one, with torrential rains and swollen rivers, but on Sunday, October 9, the skies cleared to a brilliant blue and the winds died. At dinner with friends, James E. "Ed" Hamilton, a thirty-three-year-old barefoot mailman formerly of Trigg County, Kentucky, mentioned not feeling quite in the pink. Someone suggested he might delay starting his route on Monday morning, but Ed, joking about the "medicine chest" he carried with him—a bottle of Perry-Davis Pain Killer and a spoon—was determined to carry out his duties.

The next day, shouldering his sacks, he headed south toward the Orange Grove House of Refuge. He was never seen again.

When Ed was late arriving back on his return route, friends at first were unconcerned. Since he had been feeling poorly when he left, they assumed he had probably rested for a time and would return the following day. Soon, however, the keeper from the Fort Lauderdale House of Refuge arrived with the news that Ed had never reached his place going south. The keeper also recalled a stranger walking south on the Fort Lauderdale beach the previous Monday. He was suspicious of the man's tale about crossing the river with a hunting party, believing that the stranger had used the mailmen's boat to cross to the south side of the river. A search retracing Ed's path began. In a chilling discovery, Ed's clothes, mail sack, and haversack were found dangling from the limb of a sea grape tree near the spot where his boat should have been. His underclothes lay near the water.

The inescapable conclusion was that when Ed found his boat missing, he stripped, started swimming across the 200-foot channel, and drowned.

Some friends were not so sure. For one thing, Ed was young, over 6 feet tall, a strong swimmer, and resourceful on land or water. Also disturbing was the large number of alligator tracks in the area. Fresh water from the Everglades had swollen the inlet, which still teemed with the creatures.

The grim scenario seemed confirmed a few years later when a hunting party in the area found a jawbone containing a gold-filled tooth believed to have been Ed's. Ed's friends reluctantly, sadly concluded that he had been devoured by alligators.

Barefoot mailmen continued operating until a crude road was completed from just below Palm Beach to Miami in 1893, allowing mail to be moved over land. In 1937, near the suspected scene of Ed's demise, the Lake Worth Pioneer Association installed a bronze plaque in honor of James E. Hamilton beneath the Hillsboro Lighthouse.

A Question of Courage

· 1895 ·

Women were not welcome in the practice of medicine in the 1800s, either by physicians or by most of the public. It took a special kind of woman to be willing to endure the hardships, contempt, and accusations of immorality that went along with her medical education and life thereafter. Nevertheless, some women who felt called to the medical profession persisted in pursuing the career and eventually, in answer to their needs, the Woman's Medical College of Philadelphia opened in 1850. That institution fulfilled the need for classroom instruction, but it was still difficult for women to get bedside instruction—experience caring for real, living patients. Finally, in 1869, an affiliation was arranged for female medical students to monitor clinics at Pennsylvania Hospital. They couldn't touch the patients, but they could watch.

On November 6, 1869, when thirty female students entered the amphitheater to observe hospital doctors in action, they were greeted by several hundred male students from all of Philadelphia's medical schools—with hoots, sneers, and ridicule. At the end of the session, as the women were leaving, the male students quickly formed two lines, a gauntlet, forcing the young women to pass between them while the men hurled insults and foul language. Following the females outside, the gentlemen's assault continued, accompanied by a barrage of objects that included tobacco quids and juice.

On March 13, 1879—a scant ten years later—Eleanor Galt recalled the stories of those events when she proudly received her degree, Doctor of Medicine, at the twenty-seventh annual commencement held at the Women's Medical College's Association Hall. Subsequent to graduation, Galt would pursue a medical career with the same courage and tenacity those women had possessed.

After practicing her profession for a time in New York and New Jersey hospitals, the petite, blonde doctor married a lawyer, Albion R. Simmons, in 1891 and moved to Coconut Grove, Florida. Using plans from *Encyclopedia Britannica,* the couple built a house and also a rock structure that Dr. Simmons used as an office, which still stands. Her husband became interested in making guava jelly and wine, eventually building a factory and shipping his products as far away as London.

As Dade County's first woman physician, Dr. Simmons's strength of character would be severely tested under the conditions of what was then a rough frontier. She made her rounds by horse or mule with a two-wheeled cart, encountering not only alligators and swarms of mosquitoes but also rattlesnakes and an occasional panther. When the Spanish-American War brought 7,500 troops to Miami in 1898, poor sanitation in the camps led to contaminated water supplies, with accompanying typhoid, measles, and dysentery. One soldier wrote to his folks: "If I owned both Miami and Hell, I'd get rid of Miami and live in Hell." Dr. Simmons made visits to the camps and donated badly needed mosquito nets to the hospital to cover the beds.

Even with all the challenges she faced, Dr. Simmons could hardly have expected to be involved with a notorious saloonkeeper or a shootout or any of the rest of the mayhem that occurred in the summer of 1895.

The saloonkeeper in question was the handsome S. S. Lewis. His first name was Sam but his initials were also said to stand for "Sure Shot." He was a famous marksman, the owner of a rifle he lovingly called Nancy, and he included guitar playing and dancing among his talents. On the night of July 26, 1895, a drunken fight erupted in the Lewis saloon and poolroom. Although there are many versions of the story, most accounts agree that Sure Shot, in attempting to break up the fight, was thwarted when he reached for his gun and someone knifed him. When the night ended, the only other thing agreed upon was that the affair was not over. There would be more trouble for certain.

Lewis lost no time when he spotted the two troublemakers in the street the next morning. Grabbing Nancy, he confronted them, demanding an apology. When none was forthcoming, he summarily shot both men dead. The entire town was stunned almost into paralysis. The bodies lay where they had fallen. In the confusion, Sure Shot Lewis evaded a posse and disappeared.

After a short stay in Bimini, during which almost every Lemon City citizen reported spotting him at one time or another, Lewis made the mistake of returning to Miami on a tiny sailboat. Two members of the posse, with orders to shoot him on sight, had been guarding bayfront property when they spotted him coming ashore. One of the men fired, badly wounding Lewis, who nonetheless managed to return fire. Lewis killed one man and wounded the other before crawling to a shed on the property. Other posse members soon arrived and borrowed Miami founder Julia Tuttle's boat to go to Coconut Grove and bring Dr. Eleanor Simmons back to treat the wounded posse man.

It was three o'clock in the morning when the one-hundred-pound doctor, in long skirt and high-button shoes, arrived. Swiftly, she tended to Lewis's victim, who was in great pain and had lost much blood from one neck wound and two bullet holes in his side. She made him as comfortable as she could under the circumstances and then informed the posse, "Men, I am going to the wounded man to do my duty as a doctor. Please do him no harm while I am in there."

The men of the posse watched silently as Dr. Simmons strode to the shack, calling through the door, "Mr. Lewis, this is Dr. Simmons. Can I do anything for you?"

"Yes," came the weak voice from inside. "I am all shot up. Come in quick. If anyone comes with you I will kill him."

Carrying her medical bag and a lantern, Dr. Simmons shoved the door open and disappeared, leaving the nervous posse behind. By the light of her lantern, she removed two bullets from Sure Shot's right thigh and one from his left leg. After dressing the wounds, she splinted the compound fracture of his left leg as best she could.

Her patient informed her that he fully expected to be lynched and begged her to supply him with enough chloroform so he might put himself to sleep—permanently. She refused, of course, and a few hours later, miserable with pain and thirst, Sure Shot allowed a friend to remove his guns from the shack before he surrendered.

The Lady Doctor from Coconut Grove would have been amused if she heard one male colleague's recorded opinion of women's ability to practice medicine, expounded as late as 1900: "The whole question of women's place in medicine hinges on the fact that, when a critical case demands independent action and fearless judgment, man's success depends on his virile courage, which the normal woman does not have nor is expected to have." Little did he know, Dr. Simmons and countless other women doctors had already proved him terribly wrong.

Henry Flagler's Divorce

· 1901 ·

Henry Flagler was the benevolent father of Florida's east coast. He opened up the Florida jungle by running his railroad the length of it, creating the cities of Palm Beach, West Palm Beach, and Miami. He ruled them with an iron hand although never elected to any office. His money built churches, a hospital, and schools, and installed water and electricity in the settlements. He founded newspapers and refused to stamp his name anywhere on Florida. When the big freezes of 1894–95 and 1896–97 wiped out citrus crops, Flagler lost no time helping growers recover.

He was a man who aroused envy, respect, gratitude, and admiration, but all that changed in 1901, when he was denounced from pulpits, excoriated in newspapers, and blamed for several legislators being defeated at the polls. The railroad tycoon was accused of "buying" the legislature in order to push through a law he needed to divorce his insane wife and marry another woman. Although time eventually faded some of the bitterness, his tarnished reputation never quite regained its luster.

The eighth-grade dropout had already made a name for himself before he arrived in Florida. Born in New York, Henry Flagler migrated to Cleveland, Ohio, where he joined forces with John D. Rockefeller to form the greatest industrial empire of the age, the Standard Oil Company. Although Flagler was content to allow Rockefeller's name to outshine his own, he was credited by Rockefeller himself as being the brains of the firm, the one with the most imagination.

Flagler married a lovely but frail young woman, Mary Harkness, whose health continued to fade as the fortunes of Standard Oil increased. In the winter of 1876, while the Flaglers were living in New York, doctors advised traveling to the warm sunshine and salt air of Florida in hopes of healing Mary.

At the time, Florida's population of 250,000 was settled mainly along the northern border. Except for Key West, the largest city at 10,000 people, the rest of Florida was mostly un-settled territory. Reluctantly, the scion of Standard Oil took his family to this wilderness, and in short order reported that St. Augustine was "a pesthole," Jacksonville was "awful," and there was nothing to do and he was bored. A few weeks later he re-turned to New York with his wife and family. It was against doctors' orders, but Mary refused to stay in Florida without him and Henry Flagler would not stay.

Back in New York, as expected, Mary's health continued to deteriorate, requiring Henry to hire his wife a full-time com-panion, a former actress named Ida Alice Shourds. Although his refusal to remain with Mary in a more healthful climate seems heartless, Henry Flagler never spent more than two nights away from home in their seventeen-year marriage. He preferred to spend evenings reading to his wife until her death in 1881, at which time he openly dated Ida Alice. Two years later, they were married.

By that time, his business know-how was no longer criti-cal to Standard Oil, and Henry Flagler craved new challenges. Land deals in Florida were becoming more and more attractive, leading him to his second full-fledged career in 1885. On a re-turn visit to the state, he revised his original opinion, recogniz-ing some exciting possibilities. "I believe," he said, "we can make St. Augustine the Newport of the South."

The Newport of the North was a vacation area for wealthy Americans. To pattern St. Augustine after it would require, among other things, first-class hotels. As it happened, during his stay St. Augustine was commemorating the landing of Ponce de León, a celebration that made such an impression on Henry Flagler that he began planning his first Florida hotel, the Ponce de León, which upon completion would become the largest concrete structure in the world. Although never one to spend money foolishly, he spared no expense to make his hotel the best in the world, complete with a breathtaking three-story rotunda in the lobby.

Ida Alice enthusiastically threw herself into the budding social scene, enjoying her newfound position and ability to spend money in quantities she never could have imagined. She indulged in vicious gossip and threw frequent temper tantrums, interrupting parties and balls. Flagler, however, found her charming—until her Ouija board told her the Czar of Russia was in love with her and planned to marry her upon Flagler's death. When she paid $2,000 to Tiffany's to have her miniature painted, surrounded with diamonds, then sent to the Czar (whom she had never met) it got Flagler's attention. He canceled the order and had her seen by a psychiatrist friend. As president of the Lunacy Commission of New York, the doctor was empowered to commit her to an asylum. Reluctant at first, he changed his mind, diagnosing her "incurably insane" after she injured him with scissors she had hidden.

Sometime during this turmoil, Flagler, seventy-one years old and understandably depressed, began to be seen in the company of his cousin, Eliza Ashley, along with her friend, an accomplished musician, thirty-four-year-old Mary Lily Kenan. The younger women, especially Mary Lily, helped lift Flagler from his depression. Soon, he was openly escorting Mary Lily to social functions, as aristocratic tongues wagged.

Seemingly re-energized and not content with developing his resort in St. Augustine, Flagler began planning resorts all along Florida's eastern seaboard. To service his resorts, he bought or built railroads, forming the Florida East Coast Railway, creating jobs and sparking reciprocal loyalty between him and his employees. Before long, passengers could board a train in New York City and ride all the way to Daytona. After creating Palm Beach for wealthy vacationers, it was necessary to build West Palm Beach to house workers for the resort. Next, Miami was developed, all thanks to Henry Flagler.

In the meantime, however, as gossips had a field day, Mary Lily and her family pressed Flagler concerning his intentions. He bought some time by building Mary Lily a Palm Beach home and giving her one million dollars in Standard Oil stock plus some pearl baubles worth another million. After that he started the wheels of entitlement turning.

His plan was simple. Sole grounds for divorce in New York, where he was a legal resident, and in Florida was adultery. He first changed his residence to Florida, for "business reasons." Next he petitioned the New York courts to declare Ida Alice insane; he succeeded. Finally, he had accommodating friends introduce a bill in the Florida legislature making insanity grounds for divorce. It took just two weeks from the time the bill was submitted until its signing by Governor William S. Jennings. Ten days after the bill became law, Mary Lily became the third Mrs. Henry Flagler.

Reaction was swift. Florida's conservative morality was outraged. With the exception of the Ocala *Banner,* newspapers in the state outdid one another with scathing editorials. Seventy years later, Florida East Coast Railway files revealed the truth— Flagler had made $125,000 worth of payoffs.

Some politicians who voted for the bill lost elections because of their votes. The Flaglers, ignoring gossip, editorials, and attacks from the pulpit, lived their lives much as before for the next twelve years until Henry's death, followed by Mary Lily's four years later. Ida Alice, meanwhile, having been provided for generously by her ex-husband, lived in the New York sanitarium, obliviously consulting her Ouija board, planning her wedding to the Czar. Her estate was valued at $15,000,000 when she died at age eighty-two.

Tampa Nurse Builds a Hospital
· 1908 ·

The year was 1908, a time when both blacks and whites in Florida were dying for lack of hospital care. In addition, the only public hospital in Tampa did not admit African American patients.

Dr. M. R. Winton, a prominent, caring white physician found himself grappling with a familiar dilemma. A patient in his care, a good, hard-working woman, had a tumor that needed to be operated on, and there was no time to waste. But she was black. No local hospital would admit her and even he could not change the rules.

There was nothing to be done but make the patient as comfortable as possible in her home and try to ease her pain. Accordingly, Dr. Winton enlisted the help of Clara Frye, a nurse who worked for several eminent physicians in the city and who had the reputation for being "the best fever nurse" in Tampa. Clara did what she could for the patient but, knowing her care was inadequate and that surgery was needed, she suggested to Dr. Winton that they might improvise an operating room in a cottage she knew of in Tampa Heights. He readily agreed.

The three-room cottage at 1615 Lamar Avenue, shaded by trees and surrounded by a picket fence, was Clara's own home. At Dr. Winton's instructions, equipment was brought in and the room was prepared. The patient was moved to the cottage and

readied for surgery. It was simply impossible to have an operating table moved into the tiny cottage, but Dr. Winton and the
ever-resourceful nurse didn't let that stop them. The dining
room table filled in nicely, and the tumor was removed successfully. The patient remained at the cottage while she recovered uneventfully, unaware that the bed she occupied was
Clara's own. The nurse, in the meantime, slept on a pallet on
the floor.

In a short time, three more patients came to the cottage
for treatment. Clara, seeing evidence of a real need, decided to
remain "in charge of the little cottage and make it a part of my
lifework." It seemed a fitting undertaking for a woman who
had dreamed of being a nurse ever since her childhood.

The fair-skinned Clara was born in New York in 1872, the
daughter of a white English mother and black Southern father.
Her family moved to Montgomery, Alabama, when Clara was
ten years old. When she was old enough, she traveled to
Chicago, where she studied nursing for two years. After practicing nursing for the next sixteen years in Montgomery, she re-
located to Tampa, Florida, in 1901 and married a Tampa barber
named Sherman Frye. Intelligent, reliable, and compassionate,
she soon enjoyed an excellent professional reputation. While
working for several eminent doctors, she also nursed the children of Tampa's mayor, D. B. McKay. One of those children,
Aurora McKay, was quoted as saying, "She was a wonderful
person. When we needed care, she would give it. When we
needed a spanking, she gave us that, too."

But it was with the conversion of her cottage to a hospital that Clara made her greatest contribution. In the beginning,
she had only a few beds and the facilities were primitive. Her
friend and colleague, Mary T. Cash, also a nurse, was Clara's
valued right hand. She later recalled that early on all the surgi-
cal instruments had to be sterilized in a washtub in the backyard. Although the city contributed some money for charity
patients, it was far from enough. The few paying patients were

not in a position to pay very much, so finances were always a problem. In 1916, Clara and seven other nurses solicited passersby in the downtown city streets on a "tag day," netting them $221, which seemed like a fortune. Mayor McKay once described Clara as "the good woman who gave the Negroes of Tampa their first hospital and whose kind heart kept her constantly in financial difficulties."

There were countless times when she could not pay her own bills, but somehow by 1923, with the help of a $1,000 loan from Dr. Winton, Clara managed to purchase a two-story building on Lamar Street. With the added space, she was able to care for more black charity patients, many referred to her by Dr. J. P. Lawrence, the city physician, although she worked without any official contract. Ella Chamberlain, a Tampa suffragist, was instrumental in sending many patients to Clara, some from prisons, some from the slums, all in need. Some groups donated cash and useful goods and it was all gratefully accepted.

"Here we are today in a real building with almost every convenience," Clara said enthusiastically. Then she quietly added, "But at what personal sacrifice nobody knows. There were nights when my pillow was wet with tears and my eyes burned for just one minute of restful sleep. . . ."

Charity patients usually filled the entire seventeen-bed ward on the first floor, while the twenty-nine beds on the second floor were occupied by private patients. According to a 1927 report on Negro life in Tampa, the frame building was a fire hazard, there was a persistent lack of drugs, and there were other inadequacies. It was carefully noted that Clara herself was not to be blamed.

The report must have been particularly bitter medicine, since in 1925 voters had passed a bond issue for construction of a new hospital, but none of the money was designated for African American care. According to nurse Mary Cash, Clara never turned anyone away, whatever their color or circumstance.

In 1930–31, the city of Tampa bought Clara's hospital, re-naming it the Municipal Hospital for Negroes. Dr. J. A. White, Tampa's first African American surgeon, was named the hospital medical director. But hard times would continue for the institution due to inadequate funding and the national financial disaster known as the Great Depression.

All the same, the sale allowed Clara to move into a home of her own, but according to Mary Cash, even then Clara remained poor and humble because "she never turned anybody away for a meal."

Sixty-three-year-old Clara Frye died in poverty at her home at 3303 Thirty-fourth Street on April 8, 1936 and was buried in the family plot in Woodlawn Cemetery. Years later, her old friend, Dr. Winton stated, "If I went to Heaven today, I expect the first person I'd meet would be Clara Frye."

A Chinese Man's Faith in America
·1911·

In 1911, the American Pomological Society, the oldest organization in North America devoted to fruit growing, provided a
pleasant interruption to Floridian Lue Gim Gong's lonely existence. The orange he had developed won the Wilder Silver
Medal, their highest award. Even the U.S. Department of Agriculture pronounced Lue's orange special. It made the years of
being an outsider, of loneliness and of hard work, seem worth-
while. Unfortunately, at the same time, his burgeoning reputation was also attracting unscrupulous growers trying to
capitalize on his fame and impose on his good nature.

The elderly man in tattered clothes was a long-standing
victim of tuberculosis. His vision was fading and his savings
was gone when he received the cruelest blow of all—he would
lose his DeLand, Florida home and citrus groves unless he
could pay the interest on money he had borrowed. Lue Gim
Gong, known as Florida's "Chinese Burbank," had no chance
of coming up with the money.

As a boy in Canton, China, Lue had helped plow, plant,
harvest, and market vegetables from the family fields and citrus
from their groves in the subtropical "rice bowl of China." He
had learned from his mother how to transfer pollen from the
flower of one plant to the flower of another one possessing different qualities, resulting in a third plant with the qualities of

the first two. It was this delicate skill that would one day earn him great rewards.

When an uncle who had lived in San Francisco's Chinatown told Lue how there were so many schools in the United States that even girls were permitted to attend, Lue knew he had to find a way to reach that land of opportunity.

After his uncle bought his ticket and arranged for him to stay with a friend in San Francisco, Lue's parents reluctantly gave their permission. The shy twelve-year-old spent two lonely, agonizing months on a small cargo ship, tossed about on the ocean, with bad, insufficient food, and after it was over, he could never bear to think of it again.

He was lucky to find work in a shoe factory. Many of his countrymen were indentured, owing years of wages to agents who had arranged their passage. It was not a good time to be Chinese in America. The first Chinese, brought to the United States twenty years earlier to help in the gold rush, stayed to complete the transcontinental railroad. When the railroad was finished in 1869, many of these 6,000 men were unemployed and starving. Out-of-work whites blamed the easily identified Chinese for taking jobs away. Some Chinese were beaten or stoned, and the only work many could find was in laundries or restaurants or as houseboys. The Exclusion Act was passed in 1882, making the Chinese the only nationality ever barred from immigration in U.S. history.

The owner of the shoe factory where Lue worked also owned a factory in Massachusetts, where he had previously broken a strike by hiring unemployed Chinese men from San Francisco. He was so impressed with the work of the first group that he sent for another fifty Chinamen. Lue was among them.

As the immigrants tried to adapt to the cold climate and the new language, local ministers organized a Sunday school for them. Disregarding the fact that China had a civilization 1,000 years before the Greeks built the Parthenon, the ministers considered the Chinese to be heathens who needed to be

Christianized. Townspeople wanting to help often invited the Chinese into their homes. In this way, Lue met Frances Burlingame, a teacher who was much impressed with Lue's intelligence during one of his visits. She gave him extra lessons, then invited him to stay in the Burlingame home where, in exchange for helping in the gardens, she would try to satisfy his intense thirst for education.

For the first time in his life, Lue had his own room and more books than he could ever hope to read, and he was encouraged to learn as much as he could. Before long, teacher and pupil were more like mother and son, and he was addressing her as "Mother Fannie."

Tolerated by some wealthy Burlingame acquaintances, scorned by others, Lue considered himself blessed. He missed his Chinese family, but he disgraced them by refusing to marry the Chinese bride they had chosen for him. He had become very Americanized and was subsequently disowned by his family. When Mother Fannie moved to DeLand, Florida, where the family had purchased citrus groves, Lue went with her. Within a year, Lue Gim Gong was a proud American citizen.

For the next few years, he managed the groves for Fannie and her widowed sister while he conducted experiments with fruit. Remembering those precious lessons from his Chinese mother, he combined the best qualities of two different oranges to create the Lue Gim Gong orange, which was sweet, hardy, and able to withstand sudden cold snaps. The juicy orange was also sturdy enough to adhere to the tree through the summer rains and it sold for a good price. Able to stay fresh for a long period, Lue Gim Gong oranges shipped well, making them highly competitive with California oranges.

Lue became known as "the Chinese Burbank," after Luther Burbank, a famous horticulturist. Among the unusual plant combinations Lue produced were a rosebush with seventeen varieties of roses in seven colors from a single root. A grapefruit he created that was 21 inches in circumference was too pithy for eating, but it made a delightful room freshener and its skin was perfect for candy or pickling.

With Mother Fannie's death in 1903, Lue lost his shield against the cruel intolerance of strangers, acquaintances, and even some Burlingame family members. That was when un-principled growers bought Lue's illegally-sold stock from nurs-eries who had tricked him into making misleading agreements. Those contracts cost the trusting Lue a great deal of money and led him into the dire financial straits that threatened the Florida home and groves willed to him by Mother Fannie. Fortunately, Edgar Wright, who had known and admired Lue for a long time, intervened. Wright, editor of a horticultural magazine, the *Florida Grower,* appealed to readers for help. "Nobody can know him without loving him," he said of Lue. "Let us give this meek and lowly man a square deal." Contributions were so generous that Lue was secure until his death in 1925. His faith in his adopted homeland was validated. In his will, Lue thanked the Lord for allowing him to live "in this great good country of ours."

Lue would surely have smiled when the orange, which originated in China thousands· of years ago and advanced through his humble contributions, came full circle in the year 2000, when China finally agreed to open its markets to Florida citrus.

Flying on Schedule
· 1914 ·

By any calculation, St. Petersburg, Florida, had one heck of a New Year's Day celebration in 1914—complete with a brass band, a parade, an auction, and a march into the history books. Most of the 3,000 people lining the waterfront had probably never seen an airplane before, and the clunky contraption of wood, wire, and painted cloth they witnessed bouncing in the water didn't look as though it could possibly get airborne. But the events of that day—a flight from St. Petersburg to Tampa— entitled future city leaders to install a plaque in the St. Petersburg International Airport with the proud proclamation: "The Birthplace of Scheduled Air Transportation."

The pilot, Antony "Tony" Haberstack Jannus, a young man from Washington, D.C., was regarded by aviation officials as having the experience and skill to be the flier to attempt the first transatlantic crossing. However, lacking sufficient equipment, Jannus was forced to forfeit that honor to Charles Lindbergh.

Tony Jannus displayed an early interest in mechanics, even influencing his older brother Roger to take up flying. Tony was the world's first licensed airline pilot when he went to work at the Benoist (pronounced *ben-wah*) Company of St. Louis, Missouri, teaching flying and testing planes. Roger soon joined him as a backup pilot for Tom Benoist, company owner and builder of planes.

Tony's highly publicized 1912 flight from Omaha to New Orleans in a Benoist hydroplane was the longest freight-carrying run ever, with freight consisting of several cases of Lemp Beer from the mayor of Omaha to the mayor of New Orleans. The story captured the attention of Percival Fansler, a Jacksonville sales representative for a manufacturer of diesel engines for fishing boats. Fansler, fascinated with the flight, got an idea to start real commercial flights rather than exhibitions. He convinced Benoist to supply two hydroplanes for the venture. Fansler would be the business manager, selecting routes and making business arrangements.

Fansler first approached Jacksonville officials, who flatly rejected the idea. Then he approached Tampa officials who thought it inconceivable that anyone would want to go *from* Tampa *to* St. Petersburg; they also turned him down. Undeterred, Fansler boarded a train from Tampa to St. Petersburg, a 64-mile trip around Tampa Bay and down the peninsula, which took eight to twelve hours. In those days, the same trip via steamship would have required two hours for the 21-mile journey across the bay. By automobile with hand-cranked engines on unpaved roads, it was anybody's guess. Not surprisingly, St. Petersburg officials were receptive to a new mode of transport that might considerably shorten the trip between the two cities.

Fansler contacted the publisher of the *Evening Independent,* who, in turn, enlisted other businessmen to pledge money and support. The world's first airline contract, signed ten years to the day after the Wright brothers first flew successfully in Kitty Hawk, North Carolina, included provisions for a training school for pilots.

The *St. Petersburg Daily Times* reported a new "boat" line would carry passengers across the bay in eighteen minutes and Tony Jannus, "one of the most careful aviators in the world," would soon be arriving. Since aerial accidents were quite common, subsequent stories emphasized how safe the flight would be—death would be bad for business.

The Benoist Co. disassembled a hydroplane and sent it on its way from St. Louis by rail. St. Petersburg waited. And waited. And worried. Telegraph messages flew back and forth. No one knew where the plane was. Some doubted it had ever existed. At last, seven days later, it arrived, having been mistakenly shifted to a side rail and forgotten. Frantically, the work of re-assembling it began.

The plane, made of three layers of spruce with fabric between the layers, was 26 feet long and had wings of linen stretched over 44 feet of spruce spars. With its propeller at the rear of the plane, powered by a seventy-five-horsepower engine, it could carry just two people, including the pilot, at a top speed of 64 miles per hour.

The air crackled with excitement following the New Year's Day parade. Three thousand people jammed the waterfront, tapping their toes to *Dixie* as played by the Italian Band of the Johnny Jones Carnival. At 9:15 A.M., an auction began. Although one of the partners had planned to run up the bids to $1,000, someone whispered the suggestion that it might be appropriate to allow an elderly ex-mayor, who was bidding, to make the first trip. So, with a bid of $400, former mayor A. C. Pheil was the first paying passenger of the world's first commercial airline.

Fansler made a brief speech before introducing the popular pilot, Tony Jannus. "The Airboat Line to Tampa will be only a forerunner of great activity along these lines in the near future . . . what was impossible yesterday is an accomplishment today—while tomorrow heralds the unbelievable," Fansler said. He introduced Jannus, handsome in white duck pants, dark jacket, bow tie, elbow-length gloves, and visored cap. Jannus was greeted like a modern-day rock star. Smiling broadly, the pilot promised to "always keep the maxim 'safety first' foremost in my mind."

During the speeches, a mechanic solemnly did some last-minute tinkering with the engine, and promptly at 10:00 A.M., Jannus started the engine, grinned, waved, and took off, the ex-mayor beside him, soaring into history.

As soon as the plane was out of sight, the crowd surged to the telegraph office to await word of the plane's arrival in

Tampa. Fansler later said he heard people comment that "she'd fall into the water halfway across," and many didn't believe the plane would make it into the air at all.

At 10:26 A.M., a message arrived that said, "Tony's coming up the river and there's a big crowd yelling their heads off."

The crowd in Tampa had grown to nearly the size of the one in St. Petersburg. Police had to keep them under control so cameramen could take photographs.

The return trip, begun at 11:00 A.M. with the wind pushing the plane, took just twenty minutes. Another round trip and several demonstrations that same day seemed to ensure the success of the airline. The weather was poor for flying on January 2, but Mae Peabody overcame the reluctance of pilot Tony Jannus and became the first female passenger.

With success seemingly assured, Tampa newspapers, chagrined at having lost the publicity, began taking some of the credit. The *St. Petersburg Daily Times* suggested that Tampa should "prepare . . . to accept and absorb and thrive upon the reflected, brilliant glories from St. Petersburg. . . ." The *Tampa Tribune* sniffed, "All airboat passengers have been *from* St. Petersburg and are apparently eager to get *to* Tampa."

On January 12, when the Hefner grocery store in St. Petersburg ran out of Swift meats, Fansler arranged for twenty-two pounds of ham and eighteen pounds of bacon to be delivered from Tampa within two and a half hours after the first phone call. It was the airline's first freight delivery.

The demand for service was so high that Benoist had to ship two more planes to St. Petersburg, but with a passenger fare of just $5.00 one way, the only money made was on the flight school. When the contract ran out, over 1,000 passengers had been carried, but no profit had been made. Interest faded as the "snowbirds" returned north, but Fansler, Benoist, and Jannus were satisfied that they had demonstrated that scheduled air travel was practical.

Carl and His Elephant
·1921·

If some people seem to thrive on action, speed, and upheaval of any kind, Carl Fisher would have to be their role model. From his Indiana childhood when he did headstands on fences and walked on stilts so high they had to be mounted from the second story of his mother's house, Carl's daredevil instinct was strong.

Machines, races, and excitement figured large in Fisher's life when he and his wife, Jane, first vacationed in Miami in 1910. During an inspection tour of some new property, Jane slapped at huge flies and mosquitoes and shuddered at an alligator roaring nearby, but her husband nearly exploded with glee.

"Look, honey, I'm going to build a city here!" he said. "A city like magic, like romantic places you read about and dream about, but never see. It's going to be a place where the old can grow young, and the young never grow old—the sort of place Ponce de León dreamed about."

An older man, John Collins, had run out of money trying to build a bridge to the spit of overgrown land across the bay from Miami. In return for a $50,000 loan, Collins deeded 200 acres of his land to Carl, and with another 200 acres he bought, Fisher was launched on yet another adventure and another challenge to his ingenuity at generating publicity.

Young Carl knew lean times after his father disappeared, leaving his mother, Ida, to open a boarding house in Indianapolis to provide for her three boys. Deciding he'd had enough of school, daredevil Carl left a study hall in sixth grade and began his working life sweeping a grocery store and hawking newspapers on trains. By the time he was seventeen, he'd saved enough to open a bicycle repair shop, just as the great bicycle craze was sweeping the nation.

Before long Carl was able to sell bicycles, then motorcycles, then automobiles, and his talent for whipping up promotions became legendary. He and his brothers built the "largest bike in the world," a 20-foot-high contraption that drew crowds so large police had to intervene. Carl followed that escapade with a highly publicized bicycle ride on a tightrope stretched between two twelve-story buildings.

As Fisher's interest migrated from bikes to autos, his flamboyant stunts grew more ambitious and his circle of cronies expanded to include anyone who was anyone in the fledgling world of the automobile. With two partners, he founded the Prest-O-Lite corporation, which manufactured headlights for cars and which earned the partners nine million dollars when they sold it in 1913.

But concentrating on one thing at a time was not in Carl Fisher's makeup. In 1909, thirty-four-year-old Carl married fifteen-year-old Jane Watts and built "the greatest race track in the world," the Indianapolis Motor Speedway. He rode the pace car in the first Memorial Day Indy 500.

Taking advantage of his contacts in the automobile business, Fisher was a major player in bringing the nation's first transcontinental road, the Lincoln Highway, into existence. He then pressured the same associates and promoted the north-south Dixie Highway.

All this was a prelude to his and Jane's first trip to Miami, where he was attracted to the climate and lifestyle and also recognized a promising opportunity when he saw one. Shortly after Fisher's business dealings with John Collins, the dirt began to fly. Older Miami residents shook their heads in amazement at the "damned fool" who "pumped tons of sand into a swamp" to create an island called Miami Beach. As he dredged and developed and sold lots, Carl worked to attract his rich friends in the automobile business by building a swimming casino, tennis courts, golf courses, and polo fields. When his friend Julius Fleischmann, of yeast company fame, dropped dead after one of his polo matches, Carl, never one to miss an opportunity for publicity, made sure the story was reported under a Miami Beach dateline.

Carl organized and publicized sailing regattas, deep-sea fishing trips, and speedboat races. When people, including local ministers, were shocked by Jane's abbreviated swimming apparel (no stockings and a skirt that came just to her knees), Carl was elated. Pictures of good-looking, burnished young people in bathing suits soon flooded the country, advertising Miami Beach.

With the Florida boom of the 1920s, Carl was not the only developer seeking buyers. Competition arose in Coral Gables and Boca Raton. Always on the lookout for a gimmick, he made good use of an elephant named Rosie presented to him by a friend who was the former owner of a circus. An elephant is hard to ignore under any circumstances, and Carl managed to have Rosie present for every wire service photo opportunity imaginable—pulling kiddie carts, attending grand openings, whatever. Still, sales lagged behind his expectations.

In the winter of 1920, word circulated on the grapevine that newly elected President Warren G. Harding was planning a Florida visit. Carl plunged into a spirited campaign to entice the president to Miami Beach—specifically to Fisher's Flamingo Hotel, scheduled to open in three weeks. The publicity resulting from a U.S. president's stay would ensure a full house for months, even years to come. Carl started the ball rolling with an offer to the President of a free suite of rooms, promising privacy, luxury, and relaxation and guaranteeing sunny skies for golf, deep-sea fishing, or whatever diversion was desired. He enlisted state senators he was acquainted with to put in a good word when they could—any influence he could use, he did.

Needless to say, the competition was not sitting still. For several months, developers in the Miami area made offers and waited. It looked promising. Then it didn't. Finally, when Carl's natural, good-natured optimism was deserting him, he made one last attempt, sending one of his very attractive female assistants to make a personal pitch to President Harding. Warren G. Harding was known to be a connoisseur of feminine beauty, and he reached a decision. He and his wife vacationed at the Flamingo Hotel. From the moment of the President's arrival in south Florida, Carl Fisher seldom left his side.

Flash bulbs popped, stories with a Miami Beach dateline flooded the wires, and Harding's enthusiastic public endorsement of Miami Beach was a publicity man's dream come true. One batch of photos showed the genial President on the golf course with his caddy, Rosie the elephant. Sales of Miami Beach property soared until the legendary hurricane of 1926 ended the Florida boom for everyone, including Carl Fisher.

Marjory's Poem
· 1922 ·

She would become a world-famous environmentalist before the term became popular, a feminist before that word was invented, and a civil rights activist before much of the world was conscious of such things. But in 1922 Marjory Stoneman Douglas was simply a young assistant editor and daily columnist for the *Miami Herald,* a newspaper owned by her father.

In her role as a journalist, she met many people, some famous, some seeking her out to publicize their pet projects. She was privy to stories before they went into print and to some that never did. She considered herself sophisticated and professional, but the story of the arrest and subsequent death of a young man trapped in Florida's brutal convict-lease system was nearly more than Marjory could bear.

Of course she had been aware of the existence of the convict-lease system in Florida, but she'd had no reason to delve deeply into that unpleasantness which had existed for fifty years. Crimes and punishment had gone on for a long time.

In 1570, Spanish soldiers built a prison in St. Augustine, the first in the New World outside of Mexico. From that point on, interest in the construction of a prison system faded from Florida's consciousness, as it did from most Southern states, partly because plantation owners administered punishments in private and the law never needed to be involved.

When the Civil War ended, most of the South, including Florida, was destitute, and crime among both whites and blacks was increasing. With no money to build prisons, impoverished states began leasing out groups of prisoners to private concerns such as lumber camps, turpentine camps, phosphate mines, road and railroad contractors, and farm and plantation owners. The lessee was responsible for the convicts' food, clothing, housing and medical care, although the latter was generally nonexistent. Nevertheless, it was a money-making scheme for the states. It was also a half century of relentless brutality.

Improperly clothed prisoners were worked from dawn to dusk, then chained to their beds at night. Fed inadequately, many passed out from exhaustion. For the slightest offense, prisoners were forced on runs by guards with bayonets attached to their muskets. Minor infractions were punished by beating prisoners with leather paddles or hanging them by their thumbs with their feet just off the ground until their thumbs became elongated. "Watering," another favorite punishment, consisted of pouring water through a funnel into the mouth until the prisoner suffered unspeakable agony and sometimes died. Solitary confinement was accomplished in means of 7-by-7 foot "sweat-boxes," which became "ice-boxes" in winter.

At one Jacksonville prison, three women prisoners were harnessed to a plow while other women were forced to guide the plow to cultivate fields. Women were at the mercy of guards, other prisoners, or whatever males happened by.

Florida's convict-lease system was legalized in 1877, and although all other Southern states had cruel versions of it, Florida's came to be known as the most inhumane. In a book written by a prison guard named J. C. Powell, Florida's system was called the American Siberia. But it wasn't until a tragic occurrence made news enough to capture the attention of a *Miami Herald* reporter that the rest of the country was forced to confront the ugly practice.

In December 1921, twenty-two-year-old Martin Tabert, a young man from North Dakota, set out on an adventure. He had worked hard on the family farm, saved some money, and, like his older sisters and brothers, Martin wanted to see some of the world. The adventure went well until he ran out of money in Florida. After hopping a freight train in Tallahassee, he was caught and arrested for vagrancy. Unable to pay his fine, he notified his parents, who sent funds in a letter. When the letter was returned to them unopened and stamped, "Unclaimed. Party gone," they assumed their son had found funds somewhere else and had left Tallahassee. They waited to hear from him.

In the meantime, Martin was sentenced to sixty days in a Leon County jail, and then leased to a lumber company in Dixie County. In just two months, by February 1922, the formerly strong young man was reduced to a skeletal, ailing shadow, barely able to drag himself to work. In a delirium and crying for mercy, he was beaten into a coma and died within two days. His parents were informed that he had died of a fever. It would be more than a year before they learned the truth.

Marjory Stoneman Douglas was working late when the wire came from north Florida reporting the tragedy. The vicious snuffing out of the young man's life affected her so deeply that she was unable to concentrate on her work. Pacing back and forth in front of her desk in the half-deserted city room of the *Herald,* she seemed to hear his name over and over in her mind. "Martin Tabert, Martin Tabert." A poem began to form.

By morning, the simple poem was finished, and it headed her column for that day.

Martin Tabert of North Dakota is walking Florida now.
O children, hark to his footsteps coming, for he's
　walking soft and slow.
Through the piney woods and the cypress hollows,
A wind creeps up and it's him it follows.
Martin Tabert of North Dakota is walking Florida now.

They took him out to the convict camp, and he's
    walking Florida now.
O children, the tall pines stood and heard him when
    he was moaning low.
The other convicts, they stood around him,
When the length of the black strap cracked and found
    him.
Martin Tabert of North Dakota. And he's walking
    Florida now.
They nailed his coffin boards together and he's
    walking Florida now.
O children, the dark night saw where they buried
    him, buried him, buried him low.
And the tall pines heard where they went to hide him.
And the wind crept up to moan beside him.
Martin Tabert of North Dakota. And he's walking
    Florida now.
The whip is still in the convict camps, for Florida's
    stirring now.
Children, from Key West to Pensacola you can hear
    the great wind go.
The wind that he roused when he lay dying,
The angry voice of Florida crying,
Martin Tabert of North Dakota,
Martin Tabert of North Dakota,
Martin Tabert of North Dakota,
You can rest from your walking now.

The poem was highly praised and the story received enormous attention. The *New York World* published a series of articles on Florida's convict camps that were reprinted throughout
the country. Irate editorials ran in Florida papers, generating
unfavorable national publicity and jolting civic and religious organizations into action.

Prodded by the North Dakota legislature, the Florida legislature conducted an investigation that resulted in some officials losing their jobs. Marjory's poem was read before the joint legislative meeting, with profound effect.

The man who had beaten Martin Tabert was found guilty of second-degree murder but later acquitted in a new trial. Nonetheless, the march for reform was on, and in 1923, Florida Governor Cary Hardee signed bills abolishing whipping of convicts and the convict-lease system.

Marjory Stoneman Douglas claimed in her autobiography that she considered these results the single most important thing she accomplished in her writing career.

Saving Betty Mae
· 1928 ·

On April 27, 1923, Ada Tiger, a full-blooded Seminole member of the Snake clan, was taken by concerned Indian women to a specially prepared birth *chickee* (a palmetto-thatched raised platform, open on all sides) a half-mile away from the Seminole camp at Indiantown. The woman's grandmother, Mary Tiger, delivered a baby girl, Betty Mae. Both mother and child were gently bathed by the women and put to bed, looked after, and fed nourishing meals for four days and four nights before they were returned home, where they remained isolated, except from the women, for four months. All this closely followed the Seminole way, but for one thing: Betty Mae's father, Abe Parton, was white.

Abe, a French sugar cane worker and trapper, lived nearby and was on good terms with the Seminoles, sometimes trading with them. But like any other white man, Abe was considered undesirable as the suitor of an Indian female. As late as the 1920s, young Seminole women who became involved with white men were severely beaten, sometimes to the point of incapacitating them for days, while their lovers, if caught, were killed. All half-breed babies were thought to be evil and were destroyed by either stuffing their mouths with mud or simply throwing them into the water.

Nursing hard feelings as a result of the three Seminole wars, the men of Indiantown were a particularly unyielding group. Being directly descended from the war band of Billy

Bowlegs surely added to their bitter attitude. Billy, who was credited with having started the Third Seminole War single-handedly, would never knowingly collaborate with any whites.

Betty Mae and her family managed to endure the discrimination coming from all sides until she was about five years old and her baby brother, Howard, was nearly two. That was when, late one night, a crowd of Indiantown men appeared with guns, shouting and demanding that the children be killed before they brought bad luck upon the tribe.

They failed to reckon with Great Uncle Jimmie Gopher, who had been expecting them from the day Betty Mae was born. He was a powerful man in the tribe, a highly respected medicine man. He and Grandpa Tom Tiger were prepared with rifles loaded to safeguard the lives of the children. Shouts grew louder and anger escalated until Great Uncle Jimmie shot into the crowd, hitting some of the bloodthirsty men as they fled. The children's lives were saved, but Great Uncle Jimmie was taken to jail. The arresting marshal respectfully waited before taking him away, giving Jimmie time to issue a warning in Seminole to bystanders that if the children were harmed during his absence, he would seek revenge upon his return.

Even though the children were spared, the family was no longer comfortable in Indiantown, and when Jimmie Gopher was released from jail, they moved with other Seminoles to Dania village, later the site of the Hollywood Seminole Indian reservation.

The children's father disappeared, heading west, and life was very hard for the family. Mother and Grandmother both worked in the fields, picking beans and tomatoes. Great Uncle Jimmie found some work on the reservation, and the children did what they could to help the poor-but-close family group.

Influenced by an older girl who read books, Betty Mae became consumed with a desire to learn to read. Neither the school for black children nor the one for whites would accept her, but Great Uncle Jimmie came through again. Through contact with the Indian agent, he secured a place for her in a boarding school in Oklahoma. At age fourteen, speaking no English and knowing no one, Betty Mae started school far from home and family.

For years, she had accompanied her mother, a medicine woman, when she went to deliver babies. Betty Mae was frustrated and sad when the babies died. Surely, she thought, there must be a way to save them. She respected the work of her mother and the medicine men but began to understand their limitations. The burning desire to help influenced her to become the first Seminole to graduate from high school. She then enrolled in nursing school in Oklahoma. Eventually, she headed back to the reservation, establishing a regular circuit among her people. More than once, she was chased by armed medicine men jealously guarding their territory. But in time, as more and more of her patients recovered, her reputation spread, trust grew, and she was often asked to return.

The lovely young woman was pursued by many Seminole men but finally won by Moses Jumper, a World War II hero and alligator wrestler, and they married in 1946. War memories continued to haunt Moses as he fought another lifelong battle, this one with alcohol. When he was unable to wrestle, Betty Mae took his place with the alligators, working for tips to feed her family. The marriage lasted forty-six years, with Betty Mae holding things together, herding cattle, selling crafts, shepherding her two sons and one daughter to church and school, and accepting no excuses from any of them.

When the Seminole tribe received formal recognition in 1957, Betty Mae became the tribe's first vice-chairman. In 1967, less than forty years after escaping death at the hands of tribesmen, she ran against three males and won the chairmanship of the tribe. She was the first woman Indian chief in the nation and she held the position until 1971. When she took office, the tribe's bank balance was about $35; when she left, they had half a million dollars in reserve.

Betty Mae helped found three tribal newspapers, including the respected *Seminole Tribune*. As editor of that paper, she never hesitated to criticize the tribe or the government or lecture young people about drugs or school attendance; in the process, she inspired a legend of her own.

Believing so strongly in education that she pressured not only her own children, but any others she thought needed extra encouragement, she gained a reputation as the tribe's unofficial truant officer. She was occasionally seen driving her van through pastures, terrifying cows and truants alike until she nabbed her prey, cleaned them up, and returned them to school.

As Betty Mae was becoming a legend among her own people, she was being recognized by others as well. President Richard Nixon appointed her to a term on the National Indian Opportunity Council. Named among the top fifty Indian Women in the U.S. in 1971, she authored two books and was named "Woman of the Year" by the Jewish Women's Defense League and "Pioneer Woman" by the City of Dania. She was awarded an honorary Doctorate of Humane Letters from Florida State University and was inducted into the Florida Women's Hall of Fame in 1995. The first Lifetime Achievement Award was given to her by the Native American Journalists Association.

Betty Mae was battling her own cancer when she buried her husband of forty-six years, but other awards continue to accumulate. She seems to have won both the awards and the battle.

Florida and the nation owe Great Uncle Jimmie an award of gratitude for preventing the death of that little girl more than seventy years ago.

Nazis Invade Florida
· 1942 ·

The bulging Sunday editions of Florida's newspapers welcomed the new tourist season on December 7, 1941, but by late afternoon, the tragedy at Pearl Harbor eclipsed everything already printed. Fear came to the Land of Flowers, changing Florida forever.

Like the rest of the world, Floridians had been watching storm clouds gather in Europe. After Pearl Harbor, the state speedily transformed itself from tourist mecca to military state. Airfields constructed under the New Deal became military training bases. Flight schools mushroomed in the ideal climate and topography. Hotels, emptied of fearful tourists, overflowed with servicemen and their families. Camp Blanding, south of Jacksonville, expanded to 90,000 officers and enlistees, becoming the fourth largest city in Florida. Even relaxed Key West ballooned with personnel needed to manage ship repair and maintenance. Servicemen drilled at Castillo de San Marcos, the stone fort built in 1672 at St. Augustine. Capturing all eyes, the proud women of the recently created Women's Army Corps paraded down the boardwalk in Daytona Beach.

America's entry into the war also cleared the way for German submarines patrolling our eastern seaboard to swiftly switch from observation to an offensive action known as Operation Drumbeat.

On February 19, 1942, the German U-boat ("U" for *Unterseeboot,* "submarine" in German) U-128 torpedoed the U.S.

tanker *Pan Massachusetts* off the coast of Cape Canaveral, exploding its 100,000 barrels of oil into a flaming colossus, killing twenty of its thirty-eight crew members before thousands of terrified civilians onshore. If they had entertained any lingering doubts, Floridians now knew they were at war.

Tankers and freighters carrying munitions and oil up the East Coast joined convoys heading across the North Atlantic, but the U.S. Navy was spread too thin for adequate defense. Deadly attacks continued relentlessly, destroying ships in numbers so shocking that the government hid the truth—two or three ships were being demolished every day.

Observation towers built by the Coast Guard every 3 miles along the eastern beaches were staffed in shifts by civilians, including Florida author Marjorie Kinnan Rawlings. Subs torpedoed ships day and night in view of horrified civilians, some of whom launched their own small boats in daring rescues of crewmen. Unfortunate beach walkers stumbled on burned corpses washed up on shore while overhead, women and men in unarmed Civil Air Patrol planes performed dangerous work as spotters.

After Pearl Harbor, under direct orders from Adolf Hitler, an American sabotage program was launched. *Operation Pastorius,* named for the first German immigrant to America, had two goals. The first of these goals was industrial sabotage; metal and power plants and water and railroad facilities in the East were targeted for destruction. The second goal was to incite ill feeling against German Americans, hopefully uniting them in traitorous activity while simultaneously demoralizing Americans.

The first sabotage units dispatched consisted of two groups of four men, all of whom had lived and worked in the U.S. but had returned to Germany before World War II began. One group of four was assigned to land on Long Island; the other was to go ashore at Ponte Vedra Beach, Florida.

In the Florida group was Edward Kerling, age thirty-three, who had worked in a New York packing plant and as a chauffeur. Harboring an intense dislike for Americans, Kerling became active in the Nazi party when he returned to Germany. Herbert Haupt, age twenty-two, was brought to the U.S. by his parents when he was five. His father, loyal to the Nazis, influenced Herbert to join the German-American Bund, a Nazi organization. Warner Thiel, thirty-five years old, was a toolmaker in Los Angeles, Philadelphia, and Detroit. Herman Newbauer, age thirty-two, a hotel worker in Chicago and Hartford, was sympathetic to the Nazis.

During their two months of training near Berlin, all had learned the fine points of blowing up bridges and everything they needed to know about fuses, detonators, and explosives. American magazines provided a crash course in slang and hit songs. The men received fake ID's and other forged documents at a graduation gala before boarding U-584, heading west across the Atlantic.

Four men landed at the eastern tip of Long Island on June 12, 1942. On June 17, the others rowed ashore at Ponte Vedra Beach, south of Jacksonville, in a rubber inflatable, wearing swimsuits and caps adorned with swastikas, a precaution in case they were captured. (Without military markings, they could be convicted as spies and executed. With military insignias, they could claim to be invaders and demand to be treated as prisoners of war.) Each man wore a money belt holding about $7,000 and together they pulled along four large waterproof boxes of explosives, detonators, trench shovels, and American suitcases containing American clothing, identification, and a small rubber ball. Landing unnoticed, they buried their boxes in the sand 200 feet east of Highway A1A, intending to recover them later. They headed north, pretending to be tourists playing ball in the surf and attracting no undue attention. Upon reaching Jacksonville Beach, they donned regular clothes, caught a bus for breakfast in Jacksonville, then split into twosomes and registered at different hotels.

In the morning, Newbauer and Haupt proceeded to Chicago, where they were assisted by Haupt's parents, but they made the mistake of partying with Haupt's old girlfriend and a bartender pal, who promptly turned them in to authorities. They were arrested immediately. Kerling and Thiel traveled to New York City and were nabbed by the FBI.

The New York group had landed four days before the Florida group, and its leader, Georg Dasch, had within thirty hours exposed the entire operation to the FBI. He tried to buy leniency by claiming sympathy toward America, and he cited circumstances such as pressure from his German mother and coercion from Nazi authorities because of his knowledge about America. Soon, all eight men were in custody.

Handcuffed and in leg irons, Kerling was hauled back to Jacksonville Beach to point out the location of the buried boxes. Not wanting to disrupt the possible landings of other saboteurs, the FBI maintained the strictest secrecy while munitions experts retrieved the explosives from the sand.

A trial was held for all eight men in the Justice Department in Washington, D.C. on July 8, 1942. Black curtains covered the windows. The press was excluded. At the end of three weeks, all were pronounced guilty and sentenced to death by electrocution. However, President Roosevelt commuted Dasch's sentence to thirty years at hard labor and another in the New York group, Ernst Burger, to life in prison, because of their cooperation. All who aided Haupt in Chicago were arrested, tried, and imprisoned, then deported. Six weeks after landing on American soil, the remaining six saboteurs were electrocuted by the United States Army on August 8, 1942 in Washington, D.C.

When President Truman approved clemency for Dasch and Burger in 1948, they were deported to Germany. Dasch later published a memoir, *Eight Spies Against America,* in which he reiterated his claim of sympathy to America and wrote that the FBI had double-crossed him. His claims were disputed by the FBI and he was forbidden to return to the U.S. He was by then shunned in Germany because he walked free while the others were executed.

The secret was well kept, for it was not until after the war ended that Floridians learned of the nighttime Nazi invasion of 1942.

A Small Patch of Cuba

· 1956 ·

Regardless of whether or not we ought to be there, the U.S. Naval Base at Guantanamo is to most Americans a small piece of the United States on Cuban soil. Lesser known is the fact that a patch of the Communist nation exists in one of Florida's great cities.

From the time the mortally wounded Juan Ponce de León departed Florida for Cuba, no other state in the union has been so affected by the island country 90 miles from U.S. shores as has Florida. Reverberations from Cuba's struggle for independence from Spain in the 1800s extended great distances, especially to the cigar-making enclaves of Key West and Tampa, both flourishing Latin communities. Many Floridians thought of Cuba as an outpost of Florida; some Cubans considered Florida an outpost of Cuba.

When Vincente Martinez Ybor moved his cigar factory from Key West to Tampa in the mid-1880s, it was the beginning of a population explosion and of what would become the "Cigar Capital of the World," the unique Ybor City. There, Cuban exiles created vibrant nationalist societies working passionately for the liberation of Cuba, *Cuba Libre!* While the men headed political and propaganda organizations, women organized fundraising events—fiestas, parades, picnics—and collected contributions door-to-door. Women donated everything from silver tea sets to homemade crafts; they sold or raffled the items and gave the proceeds to the cause. Women and men who held jobs donated one day's pay.

Four years after Ybor City was incorporated into the municipality of Tampa, José Martí, the "Apostle of Cuban Liberty," arrived at midnight in the driving rain at the Ybor City railroad station, eager to connect with and thank his loyal followers. Martí, a small, sad-eyed man with a gift for spellbinding oratory, was also a writer, teacher, and propagandist who worked not only for political independence from Spain, but also for social justice and the end of racism and all forms of oppression in Cuba. As early as 1892, he wrote unusual sentiments for the times—"that the campaigns of a people are only weak, when they do not recruit the heart of a woman; but when the woman rallies and helps . . . the project is invincible." Martí returned again and again to Ybor City, strengthened by the outpouring of support he received there.

One of the outstanding Ybor City women who championed Martí and Cuban independence was Paulina Pedrosa, an Afro-Cuban émigré. She managed a boarding house at 8th Avenue and 12th Street to accommodate the many unmarried men who worked in the cigar factories with her husband, Ruperto. Relatives living nearby joined with the Pedrosas and like-minded friends, responding to Martí's eloquence with organized activities in support of a free Cuba.

Paulina was tireless in her enthusiasm for the cause, and Martí regarded her as a special friend, walking arm-in-arm with her about the neighborhood. However, as time went on, it became more difficult for Martí to raise money in the United States. Spain sent spies to Ybor City to undermine his efforts, some working in the cigar factories, planting seeds of doubt as to his honesty among the citizenry. Workers began to distrust him. At one appearance, when his entry was greeted with little enthusiasm, a voice in the crowd called him a bandit and, for a moment, no one came to his defense. Among the mostly male audience was the redoubtable Paulina Pedrosa, who strode to the front of the room, angrily shouting, "If any of you is afraid to give his money . . . let him give me his pants and I'll give him my petticoat!" The men laughed sheepishly, then applauded as the grateful Martí hugged his friend.

From the time of his first visit to Ybor City, a room had always been reserved for Martí at Rubiera Hotel, but as his fame spread, it became more and more difficult for the frail Martí to rest and escape the constant, though well-intentioned, interruptions. On one particular day, following his afternoon appearance at the cigar factory, he accepted the invitation of two admiring Cubans to stay with them at their house in order to avoid the crowds. The arrangement proved satisfactory until his hosts went out one afternoon and he sampled the wine they left for him. He thought it smelled peculiar when he touched it to his lips. He spat it out, but when his doctor came by on a routine visit a little later, he found his famous patient feeling weak and faint. The doctor promptly instituted treatment, strongly suspecting that the homeowners were Spanish agents who had poisoned the wine. Martí recovered, but the doctor's suspicions seemed to be confirmed when the two Cuban men disappeared.

Word traveled like a flash through the community. Just as speedily, Paulina Pedrosa arrived, swept into Rubiera Hotel, gathered up Martí and his things, and moved them all to the house she shared with Ruperto. From that time on, there was no discussion; it was understood that Martí stayed with them, and the Pedrosas flew the Cuban flag from the gable of their house when he was in town. Émigrés kept a vigil outside in the street, hoping for a glimpse of the revered "El Maestro," watching the candle glow in his window where he worked at his desk. The Pedrosas took personal responsibility for his security during his stays, with Ruperto sleeping on the floor in front of Martí's door to ensure his safety at night. Paulina nursed Martí back to health when he fell ill from exhaustion. After they had already donated almost all their worldly goods to the cause of *Cuba Libre!*, they sold their small house, which they had acquired at great sacrifice, and gave the proceeds to the cause.

Before independence from Spain could be secured, Martí was assassinated by Spanish soldiers in Cuba, plunging Ybor City into mourning.

Paulina and Ruperto returned to a free Cuba in 1910, having struggled financially in the aftermath of a bitter strike in the Ybor City cigar factories. In honor of their service to the cause, the Cuban government provided them with a rent-free house. Ruperto was given a doorman's job, and Paulina, who was going blind, received a small pension.

Today in the heart of Ybor City is a small piece of land that belongs to the government of Cuba. At 8th Avenue and 13th Street, near where the little Pedrosa house once stood, the Park of the Friends of José Martí was created in his memory in 1956. When it was being built by the Ybor City Rotary Club, the club had difficulty raising the last $25,000. A delegation traveled to Cuba, and during a meeting with then Cuban President Fulgencio Batista, they explained their predicament. "It is an honor to contribute to the memory of the Apostle of Liberty," Batista said. "The $25,000 is yours."

And so, the site was deeded to the government of Cuba and still technically belongs to that country. Although her home burned down, a nearby plaque honors Paulina Pedrosa as "one of the great women patriots of Cuba."

Cuban Missile Crisis
· 1962 ·

Twenty-five Naval Air Station trucks lumbered through downtown Jacksonville, delivering supplies to buildings clearly marked "Nuclear Fallout Shelters." Scuttlebutt had Jacksonville at the top of the Soviet's list of targets. Children all over the state practiced what to do if the missiles came. They watched their dads build bomb shelters in the backyard, knowing that if the bad guys had their way, Florida would be wiped off the map.

In 1962, the Cold War, which had been heating up, reached a frightening level. On October 14, two United States Air Force (USAF) high-flying U-2 reconnaissance aircraft, at times flying at tree-top height, took photos in Cuba that confirmed that bases for intermediate missiles were being constructed at breakneck speed. Rumors had long circulated within Cuba about a possible U.S. invasion or assassination of Cuban Communist leader Fidel Castro. However, in the minds of President John F. Kennedy and his advisors, Soviet Premier Nikita Krushchev was attempting to alter the balance of power in the Cold War by building bases in Cuba and by arming Cubans—ultimately moving weapons closer to the United States.

Clearly, forty missiles were already in place, aimed at the U.S., able to reach as far as Washington, D.C. Under construction were bases for missiles able to destroy U.S. cities from coast to coast. Additional film showed twenty-five bombers capable of carrying nuclear bombs. Twenty-five ships sped through the Atlantic toward Cuba, loaded with more missiles and bombers.

Military experts estimated that within minutes of the firing of Cuban missiles, eighty million Americans would be dead. Quality of life for survivors was not openly discussed.

Decisions engendering possibly the most catastrophic consequences in the history of the world needed to be made by a handful of people with utmost secrecy and speed. Some experts favored immediate air and ground strikes. Some opted for political action accompanied by diplomacy. Others believed that open surveillance and a blockade of offensive weapons entering Cuba was preferable. The last option was chosen by the commander-in-chief, President John F. Kennedy, and announced at 6:00 on the evening of October 22 on national television to a solemn nation. "Should these offensive military preparations continue," he said, "I have directed the armed forces to prepare for any eventuality."

The country overwhelmingly backed their young President, as did U.S. allies in the North Atlantic Treaty Organization (NATO) and the Organization of American States.

The world held its breath, but nowhere was the crisis felt more acutely than in Florida. The state was a twenty-minute flight from Cuban shores and was expected to either be the staging area for a Cuban invasion or first to be hit by Soviet missiles.

The Florida National Guard was put on twenty-four-hour alert. Nervous citizens heard Florida described as the Achilles heel of American air defenses. Every submarine at Boca Chica base in Key West was sent to sea as the normally laid-back town converted to an armed camp. Marines with guns mingled with beachgoers on the sand as anti-aircraft missiles were sped to Boca Chica and into the Everglades. Men chosen to establish these new missile sites were rushed in without much equipment and forced to live in tents, bathe in canals, and do battle with mosquitoes.

Meanwhile, amid fear and confusion, Florida families stocked up on bottled water and canned goods, seriously considering the frenzied pitch of door-to-door salesmen selling bomb shelters. No one was sure exactly what was happening, but Orlando City Hall stocked emergency provisions, the same as they did for Hurricane Donna. Secrecy was so strict that one Orlando reporter was arrested for trying to uncover facts at McCoy Air Force Base. Tampa sporting goods stores had a run on shotguns and rifles. Only in Miami, where the train yards were filled with military equipment, was there any joy. It seemed that along Calle Ocho some Cubans believed they would be home in two days. It would be the end of Fidel, they confidently predicted.

Especially for children, it was a scary time to live in Florida. Squadrons of supersonic F-100s and F-06s tore out of Patrick and McDill Air Force Bases at all hours. While U-2s flew from McCoy in Orlando, Air Force bases in Tampa, Orlando, and Satellite Beach were on high alert, and low-level reconnaissance planes zoomed out of McDill in Tampa. Kids could hardly look up without seeing military aircraft.

Frightened parents tearfully whispered among themselves about how far children would get if they ran home from school, and men worried that they wouldn't make it from work to their families "in time." Debates raged about bomb shelters and the ethics of refusing entry to neighbors in order to sustain family members for a longer time. One man taught his children a gruesome lesson in how to use the body bags he stocked and how to dispose of bodies in case the children outlasted their parents. Families invented secret knocks to enter, keeping strangers out of their shelters. Some shelters were elaborate, with heavy, steel doors, bulletproof glass, and secret escape hatches.

Duval County children were issued dog tags, marked "P" for Protestant, "J" for Jewish, or "C" for Catholic, just in case. Most Florida elementary schools had student survival packs in citrus bags hung on designated hooks. Each pack contained canned food, bandages, and a bottle of bleach to purify drinking water after the missiles fell.

Throughout the rest of the country, people watched and prayed. Churches remained open all night, where citizens prayed for peace and for civilization not to end. The few attempts at gallows humor—"See you tomorrow, if there is a tomorrow"—fell flat. Most people were glued to their televisions, reassured by Walter Cronkite's calm presence.

A day and a half after President Kennedy ordered the blockade, the first Soviet ship was intercepted, inspected, and allowed to proceed. Sixteen hours later, a freighter was permitted to go on, but more importantly, in another part of the Atlantic, Soviet ships bound for Cuba stopped, turned, and headed home. The blockade was successful, but the missiles were still in Cuba.

While continuing the military buildup, the United States pressed Krushchev through the United Nations. There, in probably his finest hour, U.S. Ambassador Adlai Stevenson demanded that the Soviet ambassador admit before the world the placing of offensive weapons in Cuba. Prepared to wait for an answer "until hell freezes over," Stevenson displayed undisputable evidence with photos taken by the Light Photographic Squadron 62 out of Cecil Field near Jacksonville. Those pilots would each receive the Distinguished Flying Cross for skimming over the ocean to Cuba in single-pilot, unarmed Crusader aircraft, maintaining radio silence as they searched out their reconnaissance targets, took photos, and then tore out into international waters where they were met by armed escorts, hopefully before being met by Soviet planes.

Although Krushchev had ordered that no U.S. surveillance planes were to be shot down, a Soviet commander, in violation of that order, shot down a USAF plane on October 27. This action provided the Soviet premier with irrefutable evidence that the crisis was spinning out of control. The game of chicken could obviously lead to the destruction of all humankind.

When Krushchev received Kennedy's letter insisting that no settlement could be reached until all missiles were removed from Cuba, he responded one day later with a mild reply, expressing "satisfaction and gratitude for the sense of proportion and understanding of the responsibility borne by you for the preservation of peace throughout the world, which you have shown. . . ."

Kennedy answered within hours, welcoming Krushchev's "statesmanlike decision." The world breathed again. Floridians believed they had a clearer realization than the rest of the country of how terrifyingly close the world came to annihilation.

Philanthropist Solves
a Mystery
· 1965 ·

Three lean, tanned Miami Beach surfers breezed into New York City in October 1964 and unaccountably began lavishing time and attention on the American Museum of Natural History. The scheme they were hatching in their rented hotel suite would result in one of the most melodramatic jewel robberies ever recorded. With help from museum burglar alarms that had been disconnected years before as an economy measure, Jack "Murph the Surf" Murphy and his friends, Roger Clark and Allan Kuhn, removed from the Morgan Hall of Gems and Minerals a booty of twenty-two gems, including three priceless pieces so famous they were impossible to fence: the Star of India Sapphire, the DeLong Star Ruby, and the J. P. Morgan Midnight Sapphire.

The beach boys were apprehended within forty-eight hours but released on bail for lack of evidence, with the gems still missing. An eventual assist from Kuhn, who hoped for a reduced sentence, helped the police locate nine of the stolen gems, including the Star of India Sapphire, which was found wrapped in tissues in a Trailways bus station locker in downtown Miami. Still, the DeLong Star Ruby, the world's most perfect star ruby, all 100.32 carats of it, was unaccounted for, possibly being held for future ransom.

Enter John D. MacArthur, age seventy-seven, Florida's largest landowner, personal friend of Gerald Ford and radio's Paul Harvey, and brother-in-law of stage luminary Helen Hayes.

MacArthur had survived a miserable Dickensian childhood as the youngest son of a "hellfire and brimstone" self-ordained preacher who envisioned evil lurking everywhere, including in his wife and seven children. The preacher failed to provide even basic necessities for his family when he left them on frequent evangelical tours of the countryside, saying, "The Lord will provide." The Lord didn't. The children were often hungry and often black and blue. The bruises came about when their father returned and lined them up, chanting, "Repent! Repent, sinners!" and for no apparent reason beat their bare backs with a leather strap.

One brother died in a freak accident; the others escaped as soon as they could. All achieved success—the girls in marriage, John and Alfred in insurance, Telfer in publishing, and Charles in screen- and play-writing. John was so good at the insurance business that by the time he was nineteen, he had sold a million dollars worth of insurance in one year and was the company's top salesman, to the great annoyance of big brother Alfred.

In 1928, thirty-year-old John bought the Marquette Life Insurance Company, and seven years later, he borrowed $2,500 to buy Bankers Life and Casualty Company. With his second wife, Catherine, working alongside John, Bankers grew to be worth more than a million dollars five years later.

In the 1960s, John involved himself in real estate in Florida, where he built the town of Palm Beach Gardens, methodically adding to his holdings. He enjoyed getting the best of a deal, puncturing egos, and breaking rules and making up his own. Investigated numerous times by state and federal agencies, he was accused of tax evasion, false advertising, and refusal to pay claims, among other things. He survived them all.

When John was a millionaire many times over, he gave each of his employees a gift certificate for a turkey from a Publix supermarket, the equivalent of twelve dollars. Yet his employees were intensely loyal, fondly referring to him as "the Skipper." His "office" was a table in the coffee shop of the Palm Beach Shores Colonnades Hotel, which he owned and at which he kept an eye on his waitresses to ensure that they didn't waste cocktail napkins. Dressed in wrinkled pants, a ratty sweater, and a gravy-stained shirt, with a cigarette dangling from his lips, John sipped black coffee all day as he greeted a long line of people—from politicians to clergy—most of them wanting money from him, few succeeding in getting it.

John was the father of two children, but when he was the second richest man in the country, he refused financial assistance to his daughter, Virginia, who permanently deleted him from her life. He did reluctantly pay for his son Roderick's education, but he so belittled and ridiculed the young man for his love of art and literature that it was thought to have contributed to Roderick's drinking problems and psychiatric illness, including suicide attempts. Invited to dine at the White House on the occasion of a visit by the Queen of England and Prince Phillip, John MacArthur grudgingly rented white tie and tails and was quoted in local newspapers as having thought Prince Phillip was the butler. Depending on the company, he might be judged a witty conversationalist or a dirty old man. Though he didn't believe in charity, he founded the John D. and Catherine T. MacArthur Foundation, whose familiar public television logo represents more than three billion dollars given to charitable causes after his death.

He once said, "Charity is for three types. Those who believe in God, those who want to be remembered when they're gone, and those who want to impress somebody. I'm an atheist, I hope people forget me, and if I want to impress anyone, I'll paste the annual statement on the wall."

In 1965, as John D. MacArthur lunched with some advertising agency executives, he was increasingly annoyed with the ad men who were congratulating themselves for their part in his company's success, claiming their publicity was invaluable.

They seemed unaware that puncturing egos was John's specialty.

MacArthur snorted. "I'll show you how to get publicity," he said, adding that he'd do it for a lot less than they had spent.

Phone calls were made from his "office." Contacts were established. Finally, he got the information he wanted. Murph the Surf had hocked the $140,000 DeLong Ruby, probably to pay lawyers and bail bondsmen. It could be ransomed. More phone calls from the Colonnades coffee shop. More contacts. Demands for payment in advance. Refused by MacArthur. The ruby had to be returned before he would put up the money, he insisted. Agreed.

MacArthur packed $50 and $100 bills in the amount of $25,000 for delivery by a freelance writer he knew to the un-named holders of the gem. The two men then drove to a phone booth on the outskirts of Palm Beach, where MacArthur found the world's most perfect ruby parked safe and sound like a blob of chewing gum on a ledge above the folding door.

A statement was given to the newspapers that the gem would be immediately returned to the American Museum of Natural History. When reporters asked why he had done it, MacArthur smiled broadly. "Public service," he said.

MacArthur seemed pleased with himself. The American Museum of Natural History honored him for public service. Public service, priceless publicity, or both?

Dr. Cade Wins the Orange Bowl
· 1967 ·

In the early 1960s, over a cup of coffee with a football coach, Dr. Robert Cade first considered the implications of the enormous amounts of perspiration lost by football players during a game. The professor of physiology at the University of Florida in Gainesville learned that whether playing up north in the snow or at home under the blazing Florida sun, a player could lose as much as eighteen pounds of body weight in one game early in the season. He knew that no more than a half pound of fat could be burned by that amount of exercise, and with no bathroom breaks (none were ever needed) the extraordinary weight loss had to be due to perspiration.

But what other vital elements were being lost along with the perspiration? A check of existing records revealed no information on the subject, and the doctor was intrigued. With permission from head coach Ray Graves to run tests on the freshman team, Dr. Cade launched his study. (The Gators varsity was not to be experimented on, the two men agreed.)

The players' sweat was measured for volume and concentrations of sodium, potassium, protein, glucose, and other elements, plus changes in volumes before, during, and after games. Among other things, Dr. Cade and his assistants learned that as the players' blood volume falls early on, no blood is pumped to the skin for cooling. Sweat drips off, lowering blood volume even more. As the cycle progresses, blood flow to the skin becomes almost nil. The same condition continues on to the muscles, then to the brain.

With loss of perspiration, sodium in the blood goes up. Normal serum sodium is 140 and if it rises to just 150, many people become confused. At 155, almost everyone is confused, responding with difficulty to external stimuli, such as a cranky 265-pound linebacker wearing the wrong-colored jersey, looming ahead.

Tests showed players were also burning sugar, sometimes lowering their blood sugar to as low as the 40s. Normal blood sugar is 80 to 120, and as any diabetic can testify, a blood sugar level in the 40s would make one shaky, weak, clammy and, again, mentally slower and confused, a benefit to opposing football goliaths.

Dr. Cade had found three enormously important factors, each of which could have devastating effects on the abilities of a football player. For the brilliant physiology professor, the solution was self-evident—a mixture containing needed amounts of sugar and salt ingested in time to prevent the undesirable effects of heavy perspiring, but in amounts that would not affect functioning of the gastrointestinal tract.

Coach Graves gave his go-ahead to try the solution on the freshmen during a Friday afternoon scrimmage with a B team the day before a varsity game with Louisiana State University.

After an unremarkable first half ended with the B team ahead 13–0, the mystery-fueled freshmen so dominated the second half that one University of Florida player begged the opposing team to play another quarter, it was so much fun.

The impressed coach approved supplying the magic beverage to the varsity team.

That evening, Dr. Cade and his aides raided every physiology lab at the university to find enough glucose to cook up their precious recipe. They refrigerated the solution overnight, carted it onto the field in a wagon on Saturday afternoon, and passed it out to the players along the sidelines. Without going into the exact wording, suffice it to say that the liquid elicited somewhat rude descriptions as to its taste.

Although the Gators won by only a single point, they had been down 13–0 at the end of the first half and had come back to outplay LSU in the second half, allowing just one first down and no more points. From that time on, Coach Graves reversed the popular policy of the day that prohibited drinks on the field. Dr. Cade's magic potion would thereafter be a permanent fixture at all Gator games.

Attempts to improve the foul taste of the concoction with lemon-lime flavoring didn't work well, the result tasting too much like turpentine. To correct that problem, Dr. Cade sent all the way to Bologna, Italy, for a special extract he heard about that sold for $18.00 a gallon. When it was delivered, the doctor learned it had been made in the town of Frostproof, Florida, and was available in the U.S. for $1.00 a gallon.

Meanwhile, word about the exceptional results from the use of the drink, officially called Gatorade, was spreading. Gatorade was being packaged in milk cartons at the university's dairy science lab. At the last game of that season, played in Miami, a newspaper reporter noticed empty milk cartons lying on the ground and started asking questions. No, the players weren't drinking milk, he was told. It was Gatorade. The first story on the miracle drink appeared in the *Miami Herald* and from there its fame mushroomed.

Successes were repeated over and over, proving it was not a fluke. In the 1967 Orange Bowl, when the Gators outplayed Georgia Tech with flashy moves by Heisman trophy winner Steve Spurrier and a 94-yard run by Larry Smith, the reputation of Dr. Cade's invention was sealed. Georgia Tech's coach, Bobby Dodds, commented after the game, "We didn't have Gatorade, that made the difference." Dr. Cade became known as the only physiology professor ever credited with winning the Orange Bowl.

In addition, Gatorade became the top moneymaker among the patented products developed by University of Florida (UF) research, providing millions of dollars to support other research and endowments.

Gatorade was far from the only thing on Dr. Robert Cade's scientific mind. A supporter of education at all levels, he found time to substitute teach at an elementary school during a teachers' strike. He enjoyed working closely with medical students as he focused on kidney and liver disease, rheumatoid arthritis, lupus, hypertension, and diabetes. He took pleasure in his good doctor-patient relationships and often worked in his lab to search for solutions to other medical problems.

As Dr. Cade and his team began to focus on autism, they found a possible link to a child's inability to break down a specific protein in milk. Further study showed the protein produces morphine-like substances found in large amounts in autistics and also in schizophrenics and epileptics.

In 1997, Dr. Cade and his wife, Mary, sponsored building some badly needed cabins and funding several scholarships at the Florida Camp for Children and Youth with Diabetes. In 1999 they endowed a Professorship of Physiology at the UF College of Medicine, a payback, Dr. Cade said, for his first job.

The indefatigable doctor, who plays violin and viola, has long been involved in music in his community and in supporting the UF Orchestra and the Gainesville Symphony Orchestra, funding thirty scholarships for music students.

In his spare time he tends his hybrid rose garden and his collection of Studebakers. In his collection of awards and honors are the Florida Governor's Leadership Award, a Worldwide Recognition Development honor, and a Distinguished Service Award from UF. He has been named Outstanding Clinical Professor five times at the University of Florida.

But by far, Dr Cade's best-known claim to fame is Gatorade, now a staple at sporting events worldwide.

Tired Housewife from Micanopy
· 1971 ·

Spanish explorers had barely landed when the idea surfaced to slice Florida in half by constructing a canal to provide ships with a shortcut to the West Coast. This would allow sailors who feared the strange and terrifying southern tip of the Florida peninsula to bypass its treacherous coral reefs and fierce storms at sea and its hostile Indians and alligators on land. Over the years, the idea was studied exhaustively, inspiring one U.S. Congressman in the 1820s to claim he would "not think it much of a loss to the United States were the whole Peninsula of Florida sunk into the Gulf of Mexico." During the Great Depression, the project was resurrected by President Franklin Roosevelt to create badly needed jobs. It was halted once more when hydrologists doubted the canal could be constructed without damaging the Florida Aquifer and causing contamination of drinking water for central and north Florida. The project ended after ten months with just three percent of the canal finished and at a cost of $5.5 million.

The proposed canal, which always failed to meet a projected cost-benefit ratio, was revived again during World War II as a shallower barge canal. However, building materials were needed for the war and unavailable for civilian use, so the idea was once again scrapped.

After the war, Florida development exploded, with new residents arriving in droves. Soon it was hard to find any part of Florida unchanged from what had attracted everyone in the first place. The spring-fed Ocklawaha River, meandering through 110 miles of moss-draped, semi-tropical forests, with canopies of cypress and sable palms, was one place that had escaped the developers' hands. No neon signs, no waterfront condos, not a gas pump in sight.

But in 1962, pushed by Jacksonville business interests, Congress appropriated funds and, like the phoenix rising from the ashes, the barge canal idea once more sprang to life. A 16-mile section of the Ocklawaha River, pronounced the "sweetest water lane in the world" by one poet, was dammed, summarily destroying 9,000 acres of its flood plain hardwood forest. A huge crawler-crusher smashed hundreds of thousands of trees, turning one of Florida's most beautiful, rich ecosystems into shallow, weed-filled Rodman Pool, whose warm, still waters quickly filled with invasive water lettuce, hyacinths, and algae. The same monstrous contraption that felled the hardwood forest also chipped into the limestone, threatening the upper aquifer and laying waste to species of plants on the endangered list while gutting the habitat of untold animals, birds, and fish.

Rodman Pool, renamed Lake Ocklawaha by the Army Corps of Engineers, was first touted as a fisherman's paradise. It was naturally well-stocked by bass from the Ocklawaha River, but as it turned into a rancid marsh, fishing slacked off, requiring the Corps to spend substantial funds on research, poisons, and mechanical removal of the invasive plants. Species of fish slowly died off, but there were also several major fish kills resulting from low oxygen levels. Manatees were killed in the lock and adjoining structures. The dam project was a disaster by almost any criterion. Still, it was resolutely defended in the legislature by some sport fishermen and tournament organizers, as well as a few duck hunters and their supporters.

Margaret Mead famously said, "Never doubt that a small group of thoughtful, committed citizens can change the world. Indeed, it is the only thing that ever has." The words seem tailored to a group led by Marjorie Harris Carr, a self-described "tired old housewife from Micanopy," who was president of the Alachua County Audubon Society, wife of naturalist Archie Carr, and mother of five. An ecologist in her own right, Marjorie loathed controversy but realized something had to be done. She spearheaded "a small group of thoughtful, committed citizens" in a decades-long, determined lobbying and educational effort to save the Ocklawaha River.

In 1969, the Alachua County Audubon Society joined others—hydrologists, economists, lawyers, zoologists, geologists, and other scientists—to form the Florida Defenders of the Environment (FDE) to cooperate with the Environmental Defense Fund (the reversed initials were deliberately chosen) in stopping construction of the Cross Florida Barge Canal and restoring the Ocklawaha River. The alliance of scientific specialists, intent on getting the facts, effectively educated the public, press, and government. Publication by the FDE of a 117-page, carefully researched environmental impact report was a motivating force behind the formation of the National Environmental Policy Act.

The report was also instrumental in President Richard Nixon's 1971 decision to order a halt to canal construction, citing potential environmental damage. But despite support from five Presidents, most of Florida's U.S. Representatives, her U.S. Senators, and a majority of the Florida legislature, a few northern Florida Congressmen (one of whom was on the Appropriations Committee) managed to stop de-authorization of the canal—with an estimated cost of over twenty million dollars of taxpayers' money.

Marjorie Carr and the FDE were encouraged by the cessation of work but would not rest until the Rodman Dam was removed and the river restored. They stressed that such removal would eliminate the enormous costs of managing the new Rod-man "ecosystem" and that the free-flowing Ocklawaha would never require maintenance, a projected savings of twenty million dollars over twenty years.

Through the years, Marjorie clung to the principle of arriving at environmental rules based on accepted scientific principles, sticking to facts without resorting to emotional assaults. A refined, articulate speaker, Marjorie could fill a room with her laugh, then demolish the opposition with her knowledge of the issues.

"I am an optimist," she said. "I also believe that Floridians care about their environment. If they are educated about its perils, if they are never lied to, they will become stewards of the wild places that are left."

In 1990, the federal canal project was de-authorized by the U.S. Congress, the land reverted to Florida, and efforts to restore the river moved into high gear. But again and again and yet again, efforts were blocked by a few northern Florida legislators. To "honor" one state senator who was tireless in defense of the boondoggle, the dam's name was changed from Rodman to Kirkpatrick Dam.

Finally, in July 2000, conservationists had something to cheer. Governor Jeb Bush announced his support for restoration of the Ocklawaha River by breaching the Kirkpatrick Dam.

The land purchased for the canal was converted to the Marjorie Harris Carr Cross Florida Greenway, an almost continuous span of breathtaking wilderness that stretches from the Atlantic to the Gulf, preserved in perpetuity for nature-lovers.

Marjorie, Florida's First Lady of Rivers, passed away on October 10, 1997. Many fondly remember her pacing as she spoke, almost unable to contain her passion as she described the human need for such places as the wild Ockalawaha River. She once said:

I believe that our difficulty in stating our needs succinctly and persuasively can be attributed to the curious way in which we use our natural environment. For those who go hunting, fishing, boating, or camping, the task of describing what they want from wilderness is easier. These people actively do something to, or in, a natural area. For the people I represent it is enough just to be in wild places. Indeed, some advocates of more tangible activities have accused us of not using wilderness at all. Millions and millions of us do. The original landscapes of America bring us great delight, and we will defend our attitude with increasing vigor.

How the Mouse Got His Kingdom

· 1971 ·

At a glittering dinner party in St. Louis, local movers and shakers giddily awaited an announcement from Walt Disney himself that the magic of Disney would be coming to their city along with a much-needed bump to its economy.

Amid the evening's gaiety, one intemperate remark from the city's leading business tycoon silenced the congenial chattering. Augustus Busch, scion of the Busch beer family, audibly questioned the sanity of anyone who thought he could build a successful attraction in St. Louis without serving beer or liquor. Challenging the business judgment of one of the world's greatest showmen was not wise. Walt Disney, convinced that beer and theme parks shouldn't be mixed, also believed he knew more about running theme parks than someone who had inherited a beer business. The deal was dead. The quest for a perfect setting for the proposed Magic Kingdom continued.

Walt Disney was searching for a setting that would surpass the site he had selected for Disneyland. Shortly after opening Disneyland in California in 1955, Walt knew he'd made a big mistake. Immediately, others had snatched up surrounding real estate, cramming it with fast-food vendors, cheap souvenir stands, and seedy motels. Right then Walt decided that any future attractions would include enough surrounding land to provide an insulating greenway, allowing guests to totally escape the real world.

The search proceeded, secret except to Walt, his brother, Roy, and a few trusted associates. If word leaked, available land prices would skyrocket.

Back in California, Walt resumed sketching park plans in a windowless room adjoining his office, a room that had only one key—his.

As reports concerning other possible building sites came back from his team, Florida looked better and better. The climate was nearly perfect, enormous sections of land in the center of the state were used for nothing but cattle grazing, and the state's easy accessibility to the eastern half of the United States was a plus. Walt decided to see it for himself.

He and his group traveled under assumed names, and the easily recognized Walt never left the plane at refueling stops. Flying over Orlando, he made out east-west Interstate 4, under construction where it would intersect with the north-south Florida Turnpike. To the east was McCoy Air Force Base, where civilian flights had started three years earlier. Consequently, the area had excellent accessibility.

"That's it," Walt decided, kicking off an operation so secret it rivaled a Le Carre spy novel.

In carrying out "Project X," as they called it, more than fifty individual land transactions were made through dummy companies, some of them named Retlaw (Walter spelled backwards) Enterprises, Tomahawk Properties, and Latin American Development Company. New York counsel "Wild Bill" Donovan, a former chief in the Office of Strategic Services (forerunner of the CIA during World War II), provided advice and pulled strings. As land parcels sold, locals buzzed with rumors about who was buying up 24,000 acres at $180 per acre. Guesses included the Ford Motor Company and Howard Hughes, but the purchaser remained a mystery. The final price was a bit over five million dollars for 43 square miles, an area about twice the size of Manhattan island. Then the story was released.

Orlando Sentinel headlines screamed, "Disney is here!"

Secrecy paid off. After the announcement, the price for an acre of land bounced to $80,000, eventually reaching $300,000 when the Magic Kingdom opened in 1971.

If acquiring land for a fair price was a coup, Disney officials' next move was a triumph. The Florida governor and legislature acquiesced to Disney demands for creation of a special jurisdiction, the Reedy Creek Improvement District, named for the creek that runs through the area. This gave the corporation the power of an independent municipality—an unprecedented measure affording Disney control over taxation, security and fire departments, public utilities, and building and zoning codes. Rollins College professor Richard Foglesong described the jurisdiction as "the Vatican with mouse ears." The few murmured objections to zoning control and building codes were dismissed by Disney spokesmen who declared such controls necessary since they were proposing an enormous project using cutting-edge construction methods and state-of-the-art technology. One commented, "How else could you build Cinderella's Castle?" With resistance at a minimum, the measure passed and work began in 1969.

Walt, who strongly believed in environmental preservation, committed to setting aside at least 7,500 acres to be kept in their natural state and to draining swampy areas without damaging delicate ecology.

Bay Lake was drained of its unattractive brownish water, the muck that lined its bottom scooped up and combined with the seven million cubic yards of dirt dug up to enlarge the lake. Muck and dirt were used to elevate the theme park 12 feet higher than its surroundings. Bay Lake was relined, refilled with attractive bluish water, and stocked with fish.

Refusing to dig 40 miles of canals in customary straight lines, Walt ordered them curved like natural rivers. Hundreds of huge trees were moved rather than cut down, and a tree farm for the cultivation of thousands of trees and other plants and flowers was established.

Experts created an innovative telephone system, using underground cables and the first commercial fiber optic network. The most advanced electric, sewage, and water systems were installed, all controlled by a leading-edge computer system.

Future guests would not realize they were strolling on top of a bustling center of activity. Before starting construction of the Magic Kingdom, a 9-acre world of rooms, halls, and offices was fashioned into what became an underground support system for utilities, storage, dressing rooms, rest areas for employees, shops for maintenance services, electrical and plumbing centers, design and recording facilities, and an employee cafeteria.

The world's largest working wardrobe was crafted to supply costumes for living and animated figures. The world's largest laundry facility was built to wash every costume daily, along with napkins and other linens.

Another first was the installation of Automated Vacuum Assisted Collection, a waste system in which trash is collected and whisked away at sixty miles per hour every fifteen minutes through pneumatic tubes to a central compactor. Similarly, a monorail system was built to whisk guests around the park.

Construction aboveground started in 1970 with Main Street, U.S.A., Adventureland, Frontierland, Liberty Square, Fantasyland, and Tomorrowland laid out in spokelike fashion. Builders paid painstaking attention to detail, beginning first with sketches followed by scale models in order to consider appearance from every angle. Workers procured props by the thousands, added rides, and installed audio and special effects, all programmed by computers. Since castle-builders are scarce in the United States, constructing Cinderella's Castle was an interesting, 189-foot-high challenge. Additionally, Disney workers built Florida's tallest "mountain"—the 197-foot Big Thunder

Mountain—using 650 tons of steel, 4,675 tons of "mud," and 9,000 gallons of paint.

Non-Disney estimates predicted a crowd of 100,000 for opening day, October 1, 1971, and extra troopers reported for duty. When just 10,000 guests arrived at the park that day, Disney executives professed to be delighted. With no major problems, minor ones were addressed quickly. Attendance gradually increased, and by Thanksgiving of that year, parking lots filled early and had to be closed.

Within a few years, Walt Disney World became the nation's leading tourist destination and shortly thereafter, the world's. One survey showed that 70% of all Americans had visited the park, while 60% had been to Washington, D.C. Today, approximately fifteen million people visit the Magic Kingdom annually.

The Last Straw
· 1974 ·

Roxcy Bolton was used to controversy, accustomed to being belittled, humiliated, called names. *Scrappy, hero, stateswoman* —she liked those titles. But *crank, aging dragon, darned fool,* and other even-less-complimentary labels were also hurled her way. It wasn't always easy, but if the names bothered her, she seldom let it show as she went about the noisy business of pioneering for women's rights in Southern Florida.

Born a genteel Southern woman, Roxcy learned early on that gentility and white gloves had to be set aside when doors needed to be kicked in. It was 1956 when she first heard Eleanor Roosevelt speak and saw what a determined woman could accomplish. So began a lifetime of activism in which no cause was too small, no person too insignificant, to merit Roxcy's attention.

As a resident of Coral Gables, Roxcy regularly attended city commission meetings, buttonholing public officials, speaking up with passion and humor. When the mayor once threatened to have her arrested and removed from the meeting, she responded, "Go for it," calmly continuing with what she had to say. Her wisecracks and fiery comments made some people snicker before Roxcy's stern look brought the room to silence. "I hope you're laughing with me," she'd say.

When Roxcy began her career as an activist, she helped destitute mothers get child support, assisted a bag lady who slept and finally died on the steps of a Miami church, and she went to bat for a woman whose job was threatened by a younger worker with better connections. When she learned of the inhumane conditions Haitian women endured at the Krome Detention Center, she publicly threatened to take the issue to the United Nations, resulting in improvements within twenty-four hours.

In 1966, Roxcy joined with twelve other women to launch the Dade County chapter of the National Organization for Women, supporting candidates favorable to women's issues such as child care for the poor, equal pay, elimination of sex-segregated classified ads in newspapers, and maternity leave for pregnant airline stewardesses rather than the standard pink slips.

In 1969, Roxcy took on some of Miami's major department stores. Male customers in the "men only" sections of their restaurants received fast service, allowing them to return quickly to their important jobs. Women, including businesswomen also in need of fast service, stood in long lines while they looked longingly at empty seats in the men's section. It was the ultimate insult to the bulk of department store customers who were, of course, women. When polite letters of complaint failed to produce changes, the women, referred to as "Roxcy and her dolls" by one male columnist, removed their gloves. They threatened to picket, planning to supply tuna sandwiches to would-be diners standing in lines. Roxcy sealed the argument. "But men and women sleep together," she said. "Why can't they eat together?" The department stores caved in.

It was a triumph. But women won what would be an even more significant victory in 1972 when President Richard Nixon, at Roxcy's relentless prodding, proclaimed August 26 as Women's Equality Day in commemoration of women gaining the right to vote. In a note written to her, Florida's Senator Edward Gurney said that without Roxcy there would be no Women's Equality Day. Of course, success was sweet but the work went on.

Even in the 1970s, "polite" society did not openly discuss many of the issues of the day affecting women, including domestic violence. Roxcy was instrumental in founding Women in Distress, Florida's first shelter for abused women. Another thing not openly discussed and not supposed to happen to "nice" women was the crime of rape. Roxcy got people to talk about it. To bring it into public consciousness, she helped organize Dade's first Rape Task Force to participate in a march down Flagler Street in 1971. Hoping for fifty marchers, she was pleased when one hundred women showed up.

In a letter to the Miami sheriff and director of public safety, she demanded that police reevaluate their attitude regarding rape, claiming there was only one issue of importance—"the woman's body was invaded!" If a woman got off work late at night, had to ride the bus home, and was raped, people would say, "Why was she there at 11:30 at night?"

"A man robbed and beaten in downtown Miami at 11:00 P.M. does not have to explain why he was there," Roxcy said. "A woman must always explain and prove her innocence when raped. Why? Because the prevailing male attitude is rather cavalier toward rape."

Until Roxcy intervened, victims were quizzed for hours at the scene or at the police station by mostly male officers before receiving medical attention. "Police officers can no longer say they know best how to deal with rape," Roxcy informed the sheriff. "We intend to say how it is best for you to deal with this crime." What Roxcy and the Task Force wanted was a rape treatment center located at a downtown hospital where victims would be taken immediately and treated by a sensitive, knowledgeable staff. But officials took no action toward this goal.

The last straw came in 1974. The frantic mother of a seventeen-year-old rape victim telephoned Roxcy from the hospital where the girl had been refused admittance. The victim had been referred instead to the Dade County medical examiner's office, the office in charge of autopsies. The underage, traumatized young victim of a heinous crime was examined by a physician trained in handling dead bodies.

Like marines hitting the beach, the outraged Roxcy rallied her Task Force, badgering every public official at every opportunity, pleading and demanding a hospital-based treatment center. The support of county manager Ray Goode and Dade state attorney Dick Gerstein led to the Dade County Commission unanimously passing legislation to establish a rape treatment center at Jackson Memorial Hospital. It was the first such center in the nation.

The Rape Treatment Center, which opened in January 1974, received a letter of thanks from Roxcy, who said, "A Rape Center at the County's hospital can best be classified as a part of the Marshall Plan for WOMANKIND—It's overdue!!" She continued, "The ravages woman's body and mind has suffered in this country is indeed equal to suffering in war."

Patients, formerly victimized twice (first by a rapist, then by condescending police and pathologists), were taken immediately to the Center, which was located in a trailer adjacent to the Emergency Room. There they were examined by sympathetic gynecologists, received a psychiatric counseling session and routine laboratory tests before being interviewed by police. Having everything in a centralized location eliminated moving traumatized patients from one department to another and helped ensure sensitive care.

The Center, renamed the Roxcy Bolton Rape Treatment Center in 1993, is open twenty-four hours a day, weekends and holidays included. By the year 2001 the Center had provided care for more than 36,000 victims, with chilling statistics that indicate that 65% were under eighteen years of age and 45% were under eleven years. The youngest victim was two weeks old; the oldest, 105 years.

The Center tops the list of all the accomplishments for womankind attributable to Roxcy Bolton (and her dolls).

Give Kids the World
· 1986 ·

Twelve-year-old Henri Landwirth raced to his father's side when Nazi soldiers burst into their home in Belgium and put a gun to his father's head. The Nazis left that day, but they returned a few months later to take Henri's father away as the boy watched, frozen in horror. Henri also endured separation from his mother and his twin sister, Margot. He suffered in several concentration camps, including Auschwitz, once jeopardizing his life for just a glimpse of his sad, skeletal mother before she was herded with 1,000 other women onto a ship rigged to explode in the ocean. He suffered days without water, days with nothing but a few chunks of moldy bread, and he lived through a typhus epidemic in a room with twenty-five sick men. The men all died; Henri lived. He endured horrible atrocities, yet he lived.

In 1944, while American teenagers jitterbugged and screamed for Frank Sinatra, seventeen-year-old Henri barely survived a skull-shattering blow from the rifle butt of a Nazi soldier who left him for dead. Starving, delirious from his gangrenous head and leg wounds, he trudged several hundred miles into Czechoslovakia, searching for his sister.

Unaware that the war was ending, he was utterly without hope that life would ever change. But a voice inside repeated over and over, "Keep living . . . keep trying."

A Czechoslovakian couple found Henri asleep in a deserted building, took him in, and cared for him. After nearly losing his legs to gangrene, he recovered enough to go on looking for Margot. Hauling himself hundreds of miles to the town where he had heard Margot might be, his hopes shattered when he was told his last living relative was not there. Obeying a strange, inexplicable whim, Henri impulsively whistled a secret whistle—the twins' special childhood way to call each other. Incredibly, he heard Margot's answering whistle. She was there! "It was a gift," he said, "a miracle."

More than six million Jews died during the Nazi regime, but young Henri Landwirth and his twin sister were not among them.

Following the end of World War II in 1945, Henri returned to his native Belgium where he worked as a diamond cutter for a few years before leaving for the United States, sailing as a deckhand to earn his way. He had a Torah, $20 in his pocket, and a sixth-grade education, but he didn't have to worry about the future for long. Thanks to the U.S. Army, Henri spent the next two years in the service, then used his G.I. benefits to enroll in the New York Hotel Technology School, vowing to learn the business from the ground up. He cleaned bathrooms, changed linens, and worked as a bellhop and a night clerk. Nothing was beneath him as he learned the business.

After moving to Florida in 1954, Henri managed the Starlight Motel in Cocoa Beach. The Starlight was near Cape Canaveral, where the early space program was evolving. The motel served as temporary housing for the original Mercury Seven astronauts, the military, and government contractors. As the Starlight developed into *the* place to go in Cocoa Beach, Henri formed a strong network of friendships, including the original astronauts and the famed news anchor Walter Cronkite.

Working long, hard hours, Henri managed to become a franchise owner of several hotels. As his wealth accumulated, so too did his self-imposed obligation to do good with it. The ghost of the boy who nearly starved continually hovered near the wealthy hotelier whose empathy with children was boundless.

It was in his role as hotel owner that Henri discovered what he came to believe was the reason his life was spared during the dark nightmare years in Europe.

In 1986, the parents of a critically ill little girl canceled their reservation at one of Henri's Orlando area hotels. Upon investigating, Henri learned that six-year-old Amy's one wish had been to meet Mickey Mouse, but she had died before her wish could be fulfilled. Heartsick and angry that such a thing could happen to a child whose life would end before her seventh birthday, Henri learned that it usually took six to eight weeks for wish foundations to process arrangements for dying children. Six to eight weeks! Some children didn't have that long. It was something Henri had learned in Auschwitz: Every moment is precious! Someone needed to do something. Henri Landwirth stepped forward.

First Henri contacted Disney World, followed by Sea World. After that, eighty-seven Orlando hotels and the Project Mercury astronauts joined forces with Walter Cronkite and writer Art Buchwald to launch Give Kids the World, an organization designed to provide terminally ill children and their families with a free weeklong vacation near Central Florida attractions. Red tape was cut to a minimum. There were no lawyers, no contracts—just Henri asking for corporate sponsors and getting them. He accommodated 320 families the first year.

On fifty-one acres of land purchased by Henri, construction of the Give Kids the World Village sprouted, nourished by volunteering individuals and corporations. Airlines provided free flights to families, who were housed in two-bedroom, two-bath villas designed to provide a breather from hospitals, medicines, and grim treatments. A beautiful promise was born: No child will ever be turned away. Families are met at the airport by greeters who help with baggage, transportation, free tickets to theme parks and restaurants, and interpreters if needed. Leaving nothing to chance, unlimited free long-distance phone service is provided at the Village to keep in touch with families at home.

When families return to the logo- and advertisement-free Village from the parks, a toy awaits each child every day. Characters from the parks visit regularly—Mickey and friends stop by every Monday and Thursday; Shamu joins Monday evening pool parties; and Universal characters visit on Fridays. Christmas comes every Thursday with special gifts from Santa. The Village is magical for children, but something bewitching also seems to overtake sponsors, volunteers, everyone connected to Give Kids the World. Their hearts are touched. Henri says, "Goodness is contagious and it makes better everything it touches."

Parents who live with the anguish of knowing their child is terminally ill are treated to a night out during which they can reconnect with each other, but with the comfort of carrying a beeper in case they are needed.

In the Gingerbread House, families enjoy complimentary breakfasts and dinners served on furniture decorated with peppermint candies while a player piano pounds out favorite childhood songs. At the Claytonburg Park of Dreams, even wheelchair-bound guests are able to enjoy a water playground named for the Village "mayor," Clayton, a six-foot "rabbit" who visits each villa every night to tuck the children in bed. At the Castle of Miracles, a grandfather clock snores, a wishing well burps, and video games can be played for free. Guests are tempted with ice cream at the Ice Cream Palace, even for breakfast. The Amberville Train Station holds interactive trains and boats. Nature trails are wheelchair-accessible; a movie theater shows children's classics; and a volunteer staff makes it all work. Medical help is always available, since the children are very sick. Sadly, some die while in Florida. As a small tribute, village streets are named for them.

Henri, the man who started it all, looks lovingly into the children's faces and sees his own face—the boy who escaped a death-filled place to found a haven of enchantment, knowing the world is a better place because of him.

Travis McGee Day
· 1987 ·

On February 21, 1987, Travis McGee Day was declared at Bahia Mar Resort and Yachting Center in Fort Lauderdale, Florida. Songs were sung, glasses raised. Copies of the book *The Deep Blue Good-by* were presented to hotel guests. A rare bottle of Plymouth gin, Trav's favorite, was given a place of honor at the Bahia Mar bar. Amid fitting revelry, slip F-18 was dedicated as a literary landmark, permanently marked with a bronze plaque in honor of the *Busted Flush* and its owner, Travis McGee. Over seventy million books relating McGee's exploits had been sold. Well-attended conferences are still held in Trav's honor. His own popular Web site and fan magazine further attest to his celebrity.

Who was Travis McGee? He was a deeply tanned knight without armor, carelessly clad in khaki shorts and Topsiders, rugged and tender, softhearted and muscular, in the mold of Humphrey Bogart—tough, but with integrity.

A brief fling with football fame as a tight end concluded when Travis's legs were crushed in a bruising game, but the legs didn't stop him from serving in Korea. Except for occasional fleeting creakiness, he pretty much wiped the injury from his memory.

He lived aboard his houseboat, the *Busted Flush*, named for the poker hand in which he won it during a thirty-hour marathon played out in Palm Beach. In the final hours of the game, he loaned the big loser $10,000 against the boat, and then another $10,000 when that was lost, followed by the last $10,000. Finally, Travis owned the boat.

The accommodations were luxurious, if well-used. How many houseboats, even ones with a twenty-one-foot beam, can boast a shower stall nearly big enough to house a Volkswagen, not to mention a semi-sunken pale blue bathtub, 7 feet long and 4 feet wide?

Travis tied up the *Flush* at slip F-18 at Bahia Mar Marina in Fort Lauderdale, taking pleasure in water on three sides and beneath, hearing and smelling the ocean across the street, state road AIA. Bordering the ocean was the long, wide beach where assorted nonconformists showed off but generally minded their own business.

Travis spent his "off" hours doing odd jobs on the boat, hoping one day to trim the maintenance work to forty hours a week. When the sun set behind him, he propped his feet on the bow rail, listened to jazz, and drank Plymouth gin, while watching Fort Lauderdale's characters whiz by on boats, cars, bicycles, scooters, airplanes, and parasails.

He took jobs when the financial larder needed refilling. His line of expertise was that of salvage expert—that is, he recovered money on a contingency basis for desperate clients who had usually been cheated by confidence men. He doubted he would ever run out of work and he never did.

When Travis needed land transportation, he bicycled to the garage where he kept his pickup truck, arguably the world's most unique vehicle—an electric blue Rolls Royce named *Miss Agnes* in honor of his fourth-grade teacher whose hair was the same shade of blue. The Rolls had been converted to a pickup by "some desperate idiot in her checkered past," but despite her age and mutilation, she purred trouble-free along highways, oblivious to the stares of onlookers.

Friends sometimes compared Travis to the fictional Sam Spade or Phillip Marlowe, but really good friends likened him to Robin Hood with a dash of Prince Charming. Helping damsels in distress was his specialty, but almost anyone in serious trouble who needed help—male or female—could count on Trav.

Sandy-haired, with eyes the color of blue ice, Travis's scarred knuckles testified to his toughness. But in truth, he liked nothing better than the long, philosophical discussions he and his boat-neighbor, Meyer, indulged in when it suited them. Meyer was a retired economist who lived a 70-foot walk away aboard his cabin cruiser, the *John Maynard Keynes*. He was the kind of friend who actually listened, cared, and knew when to ask questions and when to keep quiet. Some of their most satisfying hours were spent ironing out the fine points of how villains had been allowed to exploit the paradise that was south Florida, whose fault it was, and how it could be prevented from happening to the rest of the state.

The exploitation of the Everglades was a large thorn in Travis's side. "Now, of course," he said in 1963, "having failed in every attempt to subdue the Glades by frontal attack, we are slowly killing it off by tapping the River of Grass. In the questionable name of progress, the state in its vast wisdom lets every two-bit developer divert the flow into drag-lined canals that give him 'waterfront' lots to sell. . . . As the glades dry, the big fires come with increasing frequency. The ecology is changing with egret colonies dwindling, mullet getting scarce, mangrove dying of new diseases born of dryness."

About the rising crime rate and loosening of the moral fiber, Trav said, "Forty million more Americans than we had in 1950. If one person in fifty has a tendency toward murderous violence, then we've got eight hundred thousand more of them now. And density alone affects the frequency with which mobs form. The intelligence of a mob can be determined by dividing the lowest IQ present by the number of people in the mob. Life gets cheaper . . . sociologists were orating about national fiber while every minute and every hour, the most incredible population explosion in history was rendering their views, their judgments, even their very lives more obsolete."

During a 1965 trip to Tampa and its historic cigar-making section, Ybor City, Travis said, ". . . they are ramming the monster highways through it. . . . They've opened up the center of the city into a more spacious characterlessness, and, more and more, they are converting Ybor City into fake New Orleans. In some remote year the historians will record that Twentieth Century America attempted the astonishing blunder of changing its culture to fit automobiles instead of people, putting a skin of concrete and asphalt over millions of acres of arable land, rotting the hearts of their cities. . . ."

So why did he stay in Florida?

"Tacky though it might be," he said, "its fate uncertain, too much of its destiny in the hands of men whose sole thought was grab the money and run, cheap little politicians with blow-dried hair, ice-eyed old men from the North with devout claims about their duties to their shareholders, big-rumped good old boys from the cattle counties with their fingers in the till right up to their cologned armpits—it was still my place in the world. It is where I am and where I will stay, right up to the point where Neptune Society sprinkles me into the dilute sewage off the Fun Coast."

Travis McGee was, of course, the protagonist of twenty-one novels by John D. MacDonald, a storyteller so convincing that fifteen years after the author's death, the novels about his fictional hero, including *The Deep Blue Good-by,* are still in print. The plaque dedicated on the first Travis McGee Day is still in place on a piling at slip F-18, and Travis's bottle of Plymouth gin, sealed and reserved, is still at Bahia Mar, where he receives about a dozen letters a year from fans who refuse to believe he's no longer there, much less that he never was.

A Granny
Goes on Trial
· 1988 ·

Popping flashbulbs added to the confusion in the little court-room packed with gurgling babies, squirming children, and moms waving signs reading GOD SAVE THE MIDWIVES and WE LOVE YOU GLADYS. Television camera crews and newspaper reporters shoved each other, struggling for the best vantage point.

The center of attention, tall, white-haired Gladys Milton, was plainly stunned to see so many of "her girls," their husbands, mothers, friends, and even their babies there to support her. There were so many. In almost thirty years she had helped bring more than 2,000 babies into the world—every baby in Walton County in 1988—and lately she was welcoming the babies of her first babies.

She had the backing of the Florida Midwives Association and the whole Florida Panhandle, it seemed.

But in 1988, the Florida Department of Health and Rehabilitative Services astonishingly "suggested" that Gladys retire or else she would lose her license. Reluctantly, she hired Coral Gables attorney Tom Sherman and there she was, in the middle of all the hubbub.

Gladys was a lay midwife or "granny" midwife to the state, meaning she was not a nurse and handled only low-risk pregnancies outside of hospitals. Before obstetrics became a profession, grannies delivered more than half of all babies born in the United States, until they were phased out by obstetricians. The women's movement of the 1960s and 1970s refocused attention on midwives, but registered nurse-midwives, licensed in all fifty states, gained the most. In Florida, only grannies licensed before 1984 were permitted to practice. Gladys was among the last of those women.

A central tenet of midwifery, "Pregnancy is not an illness," is disputed by many obstetricians, who cite complications that can and sometimes do occur. The National Center for Health Statistics points out that midwives have lower infant mortality rates, that their patients have fewer cesarean sections, and that technological procedures such as episiotomies, continuous fetal monitoring, and ultrasound, routinely used by obstetricians, result in millions of wasted dollars. Obstetricians maintain that these measures save lives, since their practices involve more complicated cases.

But in reality, for most of Gladys's life, hospital births were not possible for blacks (who were not admitted to white hospitals), while rural facilities were scarce for everyone.

Gladys, who was delivered by her own grandmother in 1924, learned to be a fighter early in her Panhandle childhood. Being a fair-skinned African American youngster with flaming red hair and a straight "A" average guaranteed that she stood out.

In time, Gladys married Huey Milton and had seven babies of her own, including twins, Elinor and Eleanor. As if she wasn't busy enough, she allowed the school nurse to talk her into becoming a midwife, an urgent need in the area.

After two years of training with two local doctors, Gladys received her license in 1959 and immediately knelt and prayed. Midwives were invariably churchwomen of fortitude and character; Gladys was no exception.

Her doctor-supervised work experience for the next five years qualified Gladys as a licensed practical nurse, and she had completed half the course work to become a registered nurse when tragedy overwhelmed her.

Her daughter Eleanor and son Kent were driving their Volkswagen home from college when they were killed by a drunken driver. Bearing the incredible agony of losing two children at once, Gladys and Huey chose to use the insurance money they received to build a small Milton Memorial Birthing Center, attached to their house.

Four months later, lightning struck and both clinic and house burned to the ground. In the confusion, a three-year-old grandson, Tyler, was forgotten until Gladys fought her way through the choking smoke to rescue him. When a patient arrived in labor, Gladys hustled her off to the nearby house of another son, Henry, who had become a physician. The indefatigable Gladys delivered the baby before dawn, graciously accepting slightly more than the customary $75 fee from her grateful patient, and then cooked breakfast for everyone.

With Huey's moral support and sweat equity, the center was rebuilt. Incredibly, though, two years later it burned down again due to an electrical problem. The Milton family and the community pitched in for another rebuilding, while Gladys good-naturedly suggested that maybe they should just keep everything in boxes so they'd be ready for the next time.

Gladys always believed that "babies are God's way of saying the world should go on," and go on she did, to a great honor in 1981.

That year, 10,000 babies were born in Florida unattended by medical professionals, and the legislature decided something had to be done. It set up an advisory board consisting of an obstetrician, a pediatrician, a registered nurse-midwife, and a lay midwife, Gladys Milton. The board created two schools for lay midwives, hoping to encourage women to use them rather than giving birth at home, alone. The grateful Florida Midwives Association agreed to have their patients seen and evaluated for prenatal care in hospitals.

But Gladys was noticing a change in her practice. More and more of her patients were educated, middle-class, and had health insurance. Consequently, obstetricians were losing patients and they were getting more complicated cases, resulting in more malpractice suits. It seemed no time before the previously supportive Florida Department of Health and Rehabilitative Services was recommending that Gladys's patients be hospitalized, even when they weren't having problems.

Tensions escalated when some of the same people originally responsible for encouraging the practices of midwives began undermining their work with clients. New fees were demanded, paperwork rejected, equipment improvements ordered. Gladys did her best to comply.

In 1987, a new patient arrived at her clinic, ready to deliver. She had seen a doctor just once, had no money for a hospital, and threatened to go home where she and the baby's father would deliver the baby themselves if Gladys wouldn't help. It was a case midwives were supposed to refuse, but Gladys, fearing the outcome would be worse if the woman delivered alone, couldn't turn her away. The delivery, a shoulder presentation, was extremely difficult. Despite heroic measures, the baby did not survive. Gladys unashamedly wept as she held the lifeless little body. She thought her heart would break when the mother hugged her and thanked her when the time came for her to go home.

Seven months later, Gladys received notice that her license was suspended, probably permanently. Gladys knelt and prayed, still convinced she had made the only choice she could at the time.

But rules were rules. In a jammed courtroom that resembled a day care center, Gladys Milton went on trial for the death of that baby and thirteen other minor "infractions." When the state's attorney acerbically requested that the babies be removed from the courtroom, the judge looked around and quietly said, "They're not bothering me." A whole row of preacher-friends uttered a heartfelt, "Amen!"

During the trial, Gladys admitted to one mistake, accepting the mother of the one and only stillbirth of her career. The judge dismissed all remaining charges, but nearly two years passed before her license was returned and she finally knew she had won.

Gladys would go on to receive many awards, including Sage Femme, the highest award from the Midwives Alliance of North America. But nothing compared to delivering her first baby after the trial, when, with tear-filled eyes, she cradled the tiny child to her heart and gave thanks to God.

Art Deco Queen Fights City Hall

· 1988 ·

The candlelight vigils had failed. The phone calls, the petitions, the television coverage—none of it had worked. The area around the Senator Hotel was cordoned off by authorities, but protesters managed to sneak through and chain themselves to the front door. TV cameras zeroed in on an elderly, frail-looking woman dressed in black—"robes of justice," she called them—attempting to fix a historical plaque on the white, curved plaster wall behind her. Viewers watched police drag her away before wrecking crews moved in. The Senator Hotel, L. Murray Dixon's sixty-room, spired 1939 landmark in Miami's Art Deco district, was about to be reduced to worthless rubble, ending nineteen months of struggle to keep it intact. In its place would be a parking lot.

Small wonder the woman felt faint. She suffered from diabetes and heart and lung problems. When her doctor was summoned, he hurriedly called an ambulance, suspecting a heart attack. The public relations director at the hospital, sensing an opportunity, notified the newspapers that Barbara Baer Capitman's heart was breaking. Perhaps—but not for the first time, nor the last. She could not, she would not, give up.

A journalist who worked for New York design magazines, Barbara raised two sons, and after the death of her husband, a professor at Florida International University, she reconnected with her roots at meetings with Miami designers. She recognized the riches of neglected, deteriorating South Beach, "God's waiting room," where poor retirees lived the best lives they could in their dismal, drug-infested neighborhood. The neighborhood claimed the oldest population and lowest per capita income in Florida. But Barbara admired the way the people congregated in lobbies and on the beaches, dancing, exercising, drinking coffee. She liked the way the low buildings encouraged camaraderie rather than isolation, as the high-rise condominiums the city was determined to build would do. She envisioned an architectural treasure that could be revived as a dynamic and diverse community. The obstacles would be wealthy, powerful developers, city hall, the chamber of commerce, the board of realtors, the Miami Beach planning board, and more.

The buildings, all needing costly repairs, stood on land potentially worth millions as the site of future luxurious high rises, with accordingly luxurious rents. There would be, as there already was farther north, a "Concrete Canyon," unfriendly to pedestrians, shading the beaches in early afternoon and deserted after dark. In 1976, when City Hall announced plans to bulldoze several hundred acres of South Beach, it seemed the wrecking-ball-obsessed developers had won. "Not so fast," said Barbara Capitman. Show time!

Barbara began organizing, and with five friends formed the Miami Design Preservation League. They concocted the name while chatting on the sidewalk outside an oceanfront villa that would become infamous as the future home and site of the unfortunate demise of fashion mogul Gianni Versace. Barbara's dogged persistence secured a $10,000 grant for a survey and plans for preservation in Miami Beach. More than 1,200 buildings were catalogued in South Beach, most within one square mile, the largest cluster of Art Deco buildings in the world. People were starting to pay attention, to see what they had never taken time to look at before. Barbara was educating them.

But the plans of the powerful were set. According to Phase II of the development project, land west of Ocean Drive was to be sacrificed for high rises. Barbara and friends successfully pressured sympathetic officials in the Carter administration to have the district listed in the National Register of Historic Places, but that was the easy part. The state of Florida's Office of Historic Preservation, whose official approval was also needed, resisted. Powerful local interests nearly derailed the effort, but after a long, acrimonious battle, the designation was won, making the crumbling buildings eligible for tax benefits. Preservationists celebrated winning a single battle in a long war.

Using her marketing savvy, Barbara instituted the first Art Deco Weekend in 1978, a fun event designed to bring people to South Beach. A partnership headed by one of her sons bought and refurbished five hotels, opening cafes on the verandas where patrons could dine while enjoying chamber music recitals, live jazz, or recorded Frank Sinatra songs. Fashion photographers discovered the incredible south Florida sunlight, and artists moved in, including the world-renowned and eccentric artist Christo, who wrapped eleven islands in Biscayne Bay with pink polypropylene. Christo and his crew hung out on South Beach, attracting even more people to the area. A television show, *Miami Vice,* was filmed on the beach from 1984 to 1989, helping in no small way to feed the frenzy.

Still, buildings were lost. It became increasingly apparent that strong local laws were needed, since private owners could continue to demolish buildings or make inappropriate alterations. Many people were involved in the fight, but the undisputed leader was Barbara Capitman, the "little old lady in tennis shoes." She did wear tennis shoes and sacklike dresses, scarcely concerned with her appearance. Her squeaky voice and speech difficulty, plus a willful, opinionated manner alienated people and contributed to the unfortunate impression she made. Better than anyone, she was aware of her failing health, and possibly because she knew she didn't have unlimited time in this world, she was persistent and uncompromising—to the point of obnoxiousness, some people thought. She made enemies of allies, feuding with everyone who stood in the way of preservation, even members of the Miami Design Preservation League. She was a "talkative, opinionated busybody." She "scared hell out of people." "She attacks people." These are quotes from her friends.

It was in 1988 that Barbara fought her last major battle. That was the year in which the fight to save the Senator Hotel, a privately owned jewel among the 800 Art Deco buildings, failed and the hotel was smashed into rubble to make way for a parking lot. By then Barbara's health was deteriorating, money troubles were mounting, and the Reagan administration had slashed funds for preservation.

However, the work never ended. New, multi-story hotels were planned among the older, small ones, dwarfing them. Other inappropriate changes were being threatened, and someone had to address them. Barbara continued her work, writing a new book and learning to create press releases on a computer. Let others rest, she thought; there was too much to do. Barbara worked until the last day of her life, March 29, 1990, one week before her seventieth birthday.

Few can argue, friends or enemies of preservation, about the economic impact of the revitalization of South Beach and its spread to neighboring areas. Today, the glittering Art Deco district is Florida's second-most-visited attraction, trailing only Disney World. The Art Deco Festival has grown to a weekend affair, attracting hundreds of thousands of fun-seekers. Investors have flocked to the area; property values have skyrocketed by billions of dollars. Bordering the north end of the district, formerly dilapidated Lincoln Road has been reborn into a pedestrian mall with one of the highest concentrations of art galleries in South Florida.

As Barbara herself wrote, ". . . today, it is hard for anyone . . . to realize that in 1976 the term *Art Deco* was barely known, and that the area, so vibrant today, was considered a disgrace to the city, because of its cheap neon lights, 'funny-shaped' buildings, and the signs along Ocean Drive blaring 'rooms $5 a week.'"

In the year 2000, the Art Deco Queen was deservedly recognized as one of the 2,000 deceased citizens important to the history of the state by the Florida League of Cities and the grateful state of Florida.

Driving Miss Diamond
·1990·

Was it life imitating art or art imitating life? Even Smiley Bruce couldn't answer that question and he was there. In 1990, when Smiley saw the movie *Driving Miss Daisy,* he could hardly believe his eyes. It was *his* life—his and Miss Diamond's—right up there on the silver screen.

Back in 1966, Smiley, a handsome, forty-seven-year-old man had started a new job as a driver and sort of an all-around "go-fer" for an elderly Jewish woman with the improbable name of Ruby Pearl Diamond. The relationship so closely paralleled the characters portrayed by Jessica Tandy and Morgan Freeman in the Academy Award–winning movie that Smiley said the movie was "sure enough about her and me." It was an award-winner in his estimation. He loved it.

It's been said that northern Florida is the most southern part of the state and, as such, Smiley and Ruby came from entirely different worlds. Smiley, an African American who had been married to Bessie Mae Bruce since 1944, was employed full-time as a night custodian. Ruby, daughter of wealthy Tallahassee merchant Julius Diamond and his wife, Henrietta, had graduated from Florida State College for Women, class of 1905. In other times, Ruby would probably have become a lawyer like her brother, Sydney, but that was not really an option for young women in the early 1900s.

For a while Ruby spent much of her time traveling, then she followed in her civic-minded father's footsteps. Julius had established the "Diamond Vegetable Basket," providing seed and fertilizer that enabled poor families to grow their own food. It was a project Ruby continued long after her father's death, just one of many ways in which she helped others to help themselves.

Ruby and Sydney both remained single and childless all their lives. A few years after their father died, they sold the family home to make way for Tallahassee's first service station. Ruby moved into Tallahassee's Floridian Hotel, remaining there for fifty years before moving to the Hilton Hotel, where she spent the last six years of her life.

When Smiley Bruce started working for her, Ruby Diamond was a seventy-nine-year-old woman accustomed to having things her way, as she'd had them all her life.

In another similarity to the movie, their relationship had a rocky beginning. Ruby was the employer, Smiley the employee. The lines were clearly drawn. For $60 a week, he was her chauffeur, but he also cooked or brought her takeout meals and ran errands for her. She had rental houses that needed overseeing and occasional repair work. Smiley supervised that work when it was necessary. Gradually, he was spending more time at the Floridian Hotel than he was at home with Bessie Mae.

In the beginning, Smiley thought Miss Diamond was prejudiced, and he was soon convinced that she didn't trust him. No matter how hard he tried, there was just no way to satisfy her. She disliked and criticized everything he did. An honest, conscientious man, he became increasingly upset and frustrated in trying to please her. Finally, as in the movie, there were one too many straws on the camel's back.

In *Driving Miss Daisy*, it was a missing can of salmon that brought things to a head. In Miss Diamond's household, the final straw came when she falsely accused Smiley of using her

Cadillac without her knowledge, an impossibility since she always had the keys with her except when he was actually driving it.

Smiley talked it over with Bessie Mae, stewed about it overnight, and, in the morning, with Miss Diamond sitting at her table, he poured out his frustration. He was quitting, he told her. He couldn't work for someone who didn't trust him.

Her face was an impenetrable mask as she sat silently thinking, staring first at the table, then at Smiley, then back at the table again.

At last, she pointed to a small leather bag on a wall shelf and asked him to bring it to her. It was, he knew, her collection of keys—the car keys and the keys to all her properties: apartment, bank deposit box, the other homes and properties she owned. She handed the bag to him. "Smiley," she said, "I'm depending on you to tend to all my things. What you see that needs to be done, you do." From that day on, as trust between them grew, their relationship changed from employer–employee to friends.

It was as friends that they took long drives in Miss Diamond's powder-blue 1963 Cadillac, visiting her old acquaintances or simply seeing what there was to see in the lush area around Tallahassee. Miss Diamond never seemed to tire of it. She once said, "There is no place in the world like Tallahassee. I have visited all over the world and have always yearned to return."

Although she generously gave to many causes, Miss Diamond could be tight-fisted, too, tipping waitresses sparingly and preferring to eat by the side of the road rather than patronizing restaurants, another similarity to Miss Daisy in the movie.

Smiley had to struggle for every raise over the years, but when Miss Diamond learned he was going to buy a $2,400 piano on installments, she sat down and wrote out a check for the whole amount, no questions asked—although she did mention that he didn't know how to play the piano. "I'll learn," he said.

She never criticized Smiley's driving except to repeatedly caution him to slow down. "If I slow down much more, somebody's going to run us over," he would answer.

Miss Diamond had always given generously to Jewish causes, as had the rest of her family. Following Hitler's destruction of so much of the European Jewish population, she was determined to help all she could to rebuild Jewish life, maintaining it as a priority for the rest of her life.

Spending so much time with Smiley had an effect on her feelings about black people, too. One white landlord who rented houses to blacks bowed to her threats of court action by installing bathrooms in the units that previously had only outhouses. On another occasion, she paid the bail for a young black man accused of a nonviolent crime. When holidays rolled around, she dispatched Smiley to buy restaurant meals for the needy, sometimes spending as much as $500 or $600.

Their relationship continued to deepen as years flew by; employer and employee became trusted friends, and, in later years, Ruby thought of Smiley as her son. At one social affair he escorted her to, another guest asked her if she was with a man. She motioned to Smiley across the room. "I have one man in my life," she said. "That's him over there."

Before she died in 1982 at age ninety-five, she had a request written into her will that her most trusted friend should raise the lid of her coffin before it was buried. She wanted Smiley to be sure it was her body inside.

"When I looked in there, I went to pieces," he said. "It hurt so bad when she died."

Among the things she left him were her father's gold watch and the powder-blue Cadillac, a reminder of the years he spent driving Miss Diamond.

Andrew Blows into Town
· 1992 ·

Year-round Florida residents are used to it. Along with humidity and mosquitoes, summer gives rise to television weather forecasters droning on about hurricane tracking charts, flashlight batteries, shelter locations, and disturbances off the coast of Africa. This prompts most Floridians to respond, "Africa? Puh-lease. I'm late for work." At least, that's precisely what they did in 1992—until Saturday, August 23, when Tropical Storm Andrew intensified into Hurricane Andrew and headed west, straight for Dade County.

Complacency gone, residents stood in lines for groceries and duct tape, boarded their windows with plywood, raided cash machines, gassed up cars, telephoned hotels, and tried to decide what to take if they had to evacuate. Wedding pictures? Birth certificates? Deeds to a house that might not be there when they returned? Those who stayed, hunkered down, never far from a television or radio in the eerily calm evening.

Shortly after midnight, the wind began to howl, things outside zapped and crackled, and the sky lit up a pretty, bright blue. As winds increased, anxiety levels rose. Huddled in "safe rooms," people no longer worried about property—they were fighting for their lives as they listened to nails pulling out from walls, roofs ripping off, glass shattering. Bodies leaned against walls that shook, dishes clattered in cupboards, and sewage leaked under doors. Ears popped painfully under Andrew's assault, as men braced their backs against doors trying to keep their families from being sucked from closets crammed with people, mattresses, and pillows. A few stole glimpses through peepholes, horrified to see trees and telephone poles snapped like matchsticks and cars and trucks flung like toys.

On the sixth floor of a building in Coral Gables, meteorologists at the National Hurricane Center, three of whom would lose their homes during the night, clocked winds at 164 miles per hour before the gauge broke. Fifteen-foot satellite dishes were tossed like Frisbees before the radar dome blasted from its twelve-story roost.

Torrential rains cascaded through roofs that no longer existed. Sometime around 3:00 in the morning, electric power went out, isolating people from the comforting presence of television personalities and enveloping them in blackness as sea water surged more than a mile inland. Waves flooded houses, cutting off neighbors from one another, completing the isolation.

Then after four long, agonizing hours, Andrew was gone, departed for Louisiana, where people had been watching television and most had wisely fled. Florida was left to recover.

Slowly, Floridians emerged, in shock, unable to believe what they saw. Neighborhoods had disappeared, completely erased. Devastation was beyond belief. Returning evacuees were unable to find their homes since familiar landmarks had vanished. Downed traffic lights contributed to traffic jams, escaped zoo animals were running wild, shreds of pink insulation draped crazily over everything. Fallen wires (some of them hot), rusty nails, and debris, glittering with broken glass, hampered movement on foot. Thirty-eight people were dead, 250,000 were homeless—more than the population of St. Petersburg, Florida. Most of the survivors wandered about dazed, searching for loved ones, shelter, water, and food. They had survived a four-hour catastrophe; another longer one was beginning.

With temperatures climbing, there was no running water or electricity for ice or air conditioning. Emergency vehicles trying to answer life-or-death calls were immobilized by debris, and the county's two rescue helicopters had been destroyed. President George H. W. Bush arrived at Opa-Locka on Air Force One and departed two hours later with promises of aid.

Although resembling a dysfunctional family before August 24, Dade County citizens, former residents of such places as Havana, Brooklyn, or St. Petersburg, Russia, connected as a community, helping each other, sharing what little they had. Those blessed with intact roofs invited strangers to sleep under them. Defrosted food from powerless freezers was cooked on charcoal grills and fed to neighbors. A man drove all the way to Georgia, loaded his truck with ice, and returned to give it away for free.

As the sounds of chain saws buzzing and helicopters thup-thupping greeted the day on Tuesday, Andrew brought out the finest in people. And the worst. Wasting no time, looters quickly emptied stores whose fronts had been ripped off. Looting for food and water was perhaps to be expected, but liquor, motor oil, and electronics went, too. One man, finding a convenience store stripped of food, took Rolaids, hoping to ease his hunger. Overworked police were spread too thin responding to life-and-death calls to stop the thievery. Signs appeared, spray-painted on shattered houses, "Looters, all good things have been removed." Guns came out of closets. With police unable to respond, every property owner with anything left seemed to be armed, on guard, and ready to shoot. South Florida needed help.

Relief efforts were in shambles, uncoordinated, snarled in traffic jams, clogged by shortened tempers fed by lack of sleep and extreme August temperatures.

By Wednesday, County Emergency Center's director, Kate Hale, begged for state and federal aid, sadly concluding, "We've had a lot of people down here for press conferences.

But . . . it is Dade County on its own." In near tears on live television, she stood up to state and federal government. "Quit playing like a bunch of kids. . . . Where in hell is the cavalry? . . . We're going to have more casualties because we're going to have more people dehydrated. People without water. People without food. Babies without formula. . . . We're about ready to drop. . . ."

But if the government was slow to respond, the rest of Florida was not. Thousands of Floridians gathered up water, diapers, and food and inched their way south on clogged highways, determined to reach suffering fellow Floridians, no matter how long it took. South Florida, land of diversity, was coming together. Police cars were loaned, portable toilets were trucked in, volunteer medics went to work to fend off epidemics. What the government couldn't do, people did, with help trickling in from the Carolinas, Georgia, and as far north as Canada. Crews from Charleston, South Carolina, reminded of Hurricane Hugo, helped repair power lines.

Five interminable days after Andrew's visit, the "cavalry" in the form of federal troops arrived. One awestruck veteran announced, "This is worse than Desert Storm." Within two weeks, 22,000 troops were deployed, making it the largest military rescue in history. Helicopters brought supplies where traffic jams prevented it; mobile kitchens were set up and marked with helium balloons to make them easier to locate; and 10,000 radios with batteries were given out.

But recovery would be slow. Homestead Air Force Base with its 8,700 jobs was gone. Dade County's giant agricultural industry was decimated, an estimated loss of $1.04 billion. Major retail department stores and food chains lost whole stores, and one entire mall disappeared. Overall, Hurricane Andrew's toll was about $30 billion, the costliest hurricane ever. Some rebuilding would take months, some years. Lessons were learned, building codes revised and enforced. Most survivors who stayed swore they would never do it again. Ever.

The good news: improved hurricane forecasting technology, giving residents more time for evacuation. The bad news: from 1960 to 1995 Florida's population tripled and is still growing, and if another hurricane with the force of Andrew hits, the destruction could be even greater.

But no one should dismiss the resiliency of Floridians. Andrew had scarcely waved a final goodbye when *USA Today* carried an advertisement from the Florida Division of Tourism stating, "FLORIDA, we're still open."

Right Stuff, Wrong Gender

· 1999 ·

"And we have liftoff, reaching new heights for women and astronomy!"

The words of the National Aeronautics and Space Administration's commentator were nearly lost as Space Shuttle *Columbia,* commanded by Air Force Lieutenant Colonel Eileen Collins, crackled and roared through NASA's glass ceiling, hurtling into the night sky over Cape Canaveral, Florida.

"You go, girl!" It was a kind of prayer that veteran women pilots and other female supporters whispered from the trembling ground at Kennedy Space Center. Eyes were glued to the fiery exhaust trail, breathing suspended, fists clenched, knuckles white.

It was July 24, 1999, almost forty years since the seven men who became this country's first space voyagers were introduced to the public. Back then, the nation was eager for heroes, tired of being beaten by the Russians ever since Sputnik first orbited the earth, beeping insolently with every pass. Project Mercury's pioneer astronauts were destined to become instant celebrities, heroes as familiar as movie stars, adored by youngsters, lionized by their parents. But while Project Mercury was kicked off with fanfare, another plan was launched in strictest secrecy, a classified program to determine the suitability of women for space flight.

In June 1959, Betty Skelton, a beautiful flyer and champion race car driver from Florida, received notice that she had been selected to be the first woman tested by NASA. It was exciting news for someone who grew up playing with model airplanes instead of dolls, who watched naval aviators flying acrobatics from her backyard in Pensacola, and who soloed illegally at twelve years of age, then legally when she was sixteen. She became a licensed commercial pilot at eighteen and a flight instructor at twenty. Partly to ease her disappointment at not being able to ferry military planes in the Women's Airforce Service Pilots (WASP) program because she was too young, Betty took up aerobatic flying. She set so many records that she became known as the "First Lady of Firsts." But she was also first to say how lucky she felt to be able to make a career of something she loved.

In spite of the thrills and excitement, Betty grew tired of the nomadic lifestyle. After returning more than one engagement ring, she recognized that she could never enjoy a normal family life if she continued the hectic schedule of air shows. So, at the doddering age of twenty-five, Betty retired from aerobatics and moved on to a more sedate realm—auto racing! She was soon setting records again.

When the call came to become the first woman tested for NASA, it must have seemed like the next logical step for a pilot with thousands of hours of flying time and one who held more aviation and auto records than anyone else in history.

For four grueling months Betty took the same tests as the male astronauts, hoping to influence NASA to include women in the program. She learned to use an Aqua-Lung for total water immersion tests simulating the weightlessness of space and the experience of performing work in a disoriented environment. The world's largest human centrifuge whirled her at high speeds, replicating conditions under which astronauts must work. She took her turn in a high-speed rotating Barany chair, a disagreeable invention designed to convince pilots, who continue to feel a turning sensation after it has stopped, not to trust their senses but to depend on their instruments instead.

Betty scored well on all the tests, but her practical side sensed from the beginning that NASA had no intention of accepting women into the program for many years to come. While she felt honored to have played a part in space history, she was wise enough to see that it might take a lifetime for women to penetrate NASA's space ceiling. Disappointed but realistic, she moved on to marriage and an executive career in advertising, grateful for her unique experience.

Her tests for NASA, however, were the subject of a cover story in *Look* magazine on February 2, 1960. The story provoked such an outcry from other women pilots who wanted to be considered for the space program that NASA succumbed to the pressure and selected another thirteen women, who became known as the Mercury Thirteen, for testing. A heavy cloak of secrecy fell, with NASA keeping the public in the dark about the testing of women from then on.

There were some things the nation didn't learn. The women had averaged more flying hours than the Mercury Seven. One, Jerrie Cobb, logged over 10,000 hours to John Glenn's 5,000. The women, undergoing the same tests as the Mercury Seven men, all passed, often scoring better than the men. Since the women had smaller body masses, they needed less support equipment that male astronauts did. Especially in those early days, this was an important consideration since thousands of pounds of rocket thrust was necessary for each pound of payload sent into orbit. Women were found to be less likely to have heart attacks and less vulnerable to pain, temperature changes, and loneliness. Dr. Lovelace, who conducted the same tests for the women as he had for the men at the famed Lovelace Clinic, thought women were better suited than men for space travel, both psychologically and physiologically. The women even set some test records, which the men were increasingly unhappy about. So unhappy were they, in fact, that they pressured NASA to cancel the women's program.

One of the Mercury Thirteen was Jane Hart, wife of Senator Phillip Hart. At his urging, a congressional investigation was launched. Included among NASA's explanations for the cancellation of the program was that pressurized flight suits for astronauts would have to be redesigned for women. Also, the men couldn't spare equipment needed to train women. However, the real catch-22 was NASA's edict that astronauts had to be jet test pilots at a time when women were not permitted to fly military jets. Since Mercury capsules were not configured anything like a jet fighter, had no wings, and had minimal controls for the astronaut, the jet-experience rule was privately questioned by some experts. That the Mercury Thirteen women had thousands more hours of flying time—more than equivalent experience—did nothing to change NASA's mind. In fact, some of the Mercury Seven men even testified before Congress, saying that they thought women were not qualified to be astronauts. However, years later it was revealed that some of these same men failed to meet NASA's own requirements; they exceeded the height limit and did not possess an engineering degree. (It turns out that NASA secretly waived these requirements in certain instances.)

On June 16, 1963, Russia again beat the United States in the space race by launching the first woman in space, Valentina Tereshkova, a parachutist with no experience as a pilot. Ground controllers ran her flight from earth. Twelve years later the Kennedy Space Center launched the first American woman, Dr. Sally Ride, a mission specialist rather than a pilot. The launch of a female pilot took another twelve years. It was a full thirty-six years from the time Tereshkova was launched to the time Colonel Eileen Collins roared into history as America's first female mission commander.

Betty Skelton, still interested in flying, space, and fast cars, was named to the Florida Women's Hall of Fame in 1993. She watches U.S. space shots from her living room window in Florida, still wishing she could be on board.

Butterflies and Ballots

· 2000 ·

Massachusetts Institute of Technology meteorologist Edward Lorenz first described the "Butterfly Effect," the idea that a butterfly stirring the air in China in March might change the weather over the Atlantic Ocean in August. Scientists characterize the Butterfly Effect as the "sensitive dependence of outcomes on initial conditions." To the rest of us, it simply means the enormous, unexpected results of seemingly insignificant activities, and it must surely apply to the closest election in American history—the presidential election of 2000.

Among the "initial conditions" of Election 2000 was use of the Votomatic machine by most Floridians and by one-third of all Americans. Punch-card technology used in the Votomatic machines dated from 1890 and was so unreliable that officials had for some time acknowledged and accepted a loss of 2% of votes in every election due to *undervotes* (ballots with no candidate voted for) or *overvotes* (ballots marked for more than one candidate). In Palm Beach County, where a cheaper version of the problem-plagued Votomatic was in use, machines were so defective or damaged that no amount of care or intelligence on the part of voters would have prevented lost votes, regardless of disparaging appraisals by other citizens of the mental capabilities of Florida voters.

Before Election 2000, scarcely any American had ever heard of *chads,* the tiny pieces of paper punched out by the stylus when a voter votes. After the election, most Americans learned more than they cared to know about hanging chads, dimpled chads, and pregnant chads. Few voters knew hanging chads could fall off, become stuck in vote-reading machines, or stick in other holes in the same card or in other voters' cards, causing incorrect tabulation. As far back as 1988, the National Institute of Standards and Technology urged that Votomatic punch cards be eliminated. That same year, when they were suspect in the Miami–Dade County Florida senatorial contest, voting machine manufacturers blamed election supervisors for not educating the public. Election supervisors blamed the public for making errors, while the public was unaware that special knowledge was needed to vote. One political science professor suggested that casting a vote should not be rocket science.

Other "initial conditions" affecting the outcome of the election in Florida were illegal votes cast by felons, unregistered voters who swore they were eligible but weren't, and some who voted by absentee ballot and then again in person at the polls. A large voter turnout led overwhelmed poll workers to accept a surprising number of questionable votes. When workers sought help, they faced jammed phone lines at election supervisors' offices.

Furthermore, the workers were put to work after only four or five hours of training and were paid minimum wages to work long, grueling hours. Many were elderly, sometimes frail, but were usually principled, honest, and patriotic.

As long as a year before Election 2000, another "initial condition" originated with Florida Governor Jeb Bush's "One Florida Initiative," a program that ended affirmative action in granting state contracts and in higher education. By failing to consult with black leadership and refusing to meet with black legislators on the matter, the governor so aroused the ire of

African American Floridians that they turned out in record numbers to vote against his brother in the presidential election—60% more than had voted in 1996. The problem was that many were first-time voters and no one had shown them how to vote. Most had too much pride to ask for help; some did and were rebuffed by poll workers. Additionally, many new Haitian American citizens had language difficulties that hampered their ability to vote correctly. Accusations of unauthorized roadblocks by police in black voting districts surfaced and were denied, causing Jesse Jackson to fly into the state to rally his people, convinced they were being disenfranchised.

Probably the most significant "initial condition" came into existence when, six months before the election, an average person in a boilerplate job—the Palm Beach County Supervisor of Elections—began preparations for Election 2000. She was responsible for staffing 531 precincts, training 4,000 poll workers, checking qualifications of candidates, and, in spite of having no training in the field, choosing the ballot design. The design that was approved quite likely tipped the balance in votes in the county and was considered by some as the most important component in installing the man who lost the popular vote into the highest office in the nation.

The unusually large number of presidential candidates on the ballot—ten in all—would have been crowded on a one-page ballot, requiring type that Palm Beach County Supervisor Theresa LePore considered too small for the large elderly population to see easily. Instead, she chose a design with the candidates' names split on two pages. With that small action, the butterfly ballot was born—the butterfly flapped its wings, stirring the air toward enormous, unanticipated consequences.

In fairness, candidates, political party bosses, and the general public were shown the ballot, and no complaints were registered. The problem was that the ballots as shown to all those people did not show the punch holes between the two pages, which was exactly what many found confusing when confronted with the real thing. George W. Bush's name topped the left page, with Albert Gore's just below. Pat Buchanan's name was on the right page, between the two, which meant that although Gore's name was second from the top of the page, the hole that had to be punched for him was third from the top. Had the ballot been user-tested, which it was not, its flaws would have been apparent immediately. As such, the poor design of the ballot was a most important "initial condition" affecting the extraordinary events that followed. By 9:00 A.M. on election day, phones in LePore's office started ringing. By 10:30, people were arriving in person, all complaining about the ballot, some in tears.

After comparing notes with neighbors, many elderly Jewish voters suspected or knew they had mistakenly voted for Buchanan, whom they perceived to be an anti-Semite. Buchanan, the Reform Party candidate, had accumulated such an amazing number of votes in the Jewish community, one resident said, "Yasser Arafat could have gotten more votes here." A rabbi added, "If Palm Beach is a Buchanan stronghold, then so is my synagogue." People in their eighties—some Holocaust survivors who had waited all their lives to vote for a Jewish candidate—knew their vote for Joe Leiberman, Gore's running mate for vice-president, was lost.

LePore's reaction? She understood that the ballot might have caused some confusion, she said, but voters needed to take some responsibility.

Then the race for the presidency came down to a dead heat. Just a few hundred votes would decide the election in Florida and—because of the state's large number of electoral votes—in the nation. For thirty-six days, Americans watched the two main political candidates mount claims and counterclaims, file suits and countersuits, and issue challenges and demand recounts in a bizarre display of political science that ended with the decision of the U.S. Supreme Court in favor of George W. Bush.

Have the butterfly wings stopped flapping? Hardly. His-
torically, just one new life-tenured presidential appointee to a
sharply divided U.S. Supreme Court can profoundly influence
the direction of the country for many years beyond any president's administration. The fundamental rights of all citizens are
affected by far-reaching judicial decisions.

Additionally, the presidential election of 2000 led to the
realization that the voting process in the nation is terribly
flawed. Florida has led the way in replacing unreliable voting
machines, redesigning ballots, and retraining poll workers and
their supervisors—the start of a decade-long process to up-
grade voting equipment and procedures nationwide in order to
carry out the will of the people.

The gentle wings of the butterfly ballot continue to flap.

Space Chimps Retire
· 2001 ·

In the mid-1950s the United States Air Force authorized hunters to capture sixty-five baby chimpanzees from the wilds of Africa. Knowing that a strong mother–infant bond existed, hunters first stalked and then killed the mother chimpanzees before tying the screaming babies to poles and carrying them to the coast, where they were crated and shipped across the ocean. One out of ten chimps survived to arrive in the United States, where the Air Force took control of them. Experiments began, some spinning the unfortunate babies in giant centrifuges to test their reaction to enormous G forces, others measuring the length of time it took before the chimps lost consciousness in a decompression chamber.

To determine whether or not mental facility would be affected by conditions during space launches, weightlessness, and re-entry, the chimps were rigorously trained and tested using a system of rewards and punishments for performance on a simulated panel with levers and lights. Correct responses earned banana pellets; incorrect ones brought a mild electrical shock to their feet.

By 1961, NASA was ready. On January 31, a three-year-old chimp named Ham was strapped onto his couch in the Mercury capsule. After a six-hour delay, the enormous Redstone rocket rumbled and blasted into space, almost immediately malfunctioning. The capsule, expected to travel at 4,200 miles per hour, instead reached 5,800 miles per hour, exposing Ham to 18G forces, instead of 11Gs, as predicted. Ham, however, performed his duties perfectly, returned to earthly applause, and was featured on the cover of *Life* magazine. Three months later, human astronaut Alan Shepard followed Ham into space.

To get a capsule into orbit was another matter, requiring a more powerful rocket. Testing the new Atlas rocket, five-year-old chimp Enos, first in his class, was launched on November 29, 1961. After numerous glitches during liftoff and a shaky first orbit, several malfunctions caused the cabin temperature to rise and fuel usage to increase rapidly. The capsule wobbled and the reward–punishment system flipped into reverse. The "dumb beast" who had trained for over a year should have performed incorrectly due to the topsy-turvy delivery of banana pellets and shocks. But Enos did what he knew was right, despite receiving a shock for every correct move he made. The third orbit was aborted. Enos was saved from certain incineration when he was removed from the capsule, which registered 106 degrees Fahrenheit.

NASA made 250 adjustments to improve the spacecraft based on what was learned during the Ham and Enos flights. John Glenn was launched ten months later.

While some chimps were not trained for flight, all were tested in painful, frightening ways to gauge the dangerous or unpleasant effects encountered in space travel.

Human astronauts became instant heroes, to an extent that surprised even NASA. Ticker-tape parades, television interviews, lucrative offers, and adoration were showered on the Mercury Seven astronauts while the "chimponauts" were reassigned to "hazardous mission environment"—testing seat belts. Then, in 1970, the Air Force began leasing the chimps out for biomedical research that involved infecting them with AIDS or hepatitis. That was eventually determined to be useless since chimps reacted differently than humans. In the meantime, however, another group of former space chimps had their teeth smashed in with a steel ball to provide experience in reconstructive procedures for dental students. The chimps, social animals who live in groups and have a life span of fifty years or more, were housed in too-small cages and denied access to the outdoors, companions, or diversions of any kind.

According to famous primatologist Jane Goodall, "Research shows that chimps think, feel, and communicate in ways almost identical to man." She has proven that they use tools, have emotions, and play with toys. They kiss, embrace, and have a dark side, as humans do.

Fifty years ago, about one million chimpanzees lived in the African wilds. There are perhaps 150,000 left there today. Of the 2,400 chimps who live in the U.S., 1,700 are being used for biomedical testing; the other 700 are in zoos or in the entertainment industry—a sad fate for our closest living relatives, who share all but 1.4% of our DNA.

Protests by Goodall and Roger Fouts, pioneer of chimpanzee language research, and John Glenn, former astronaut and senator from Ohio, went nowhere. Instead, the Air Force transferred the chimps to the Coulston Foundation, an organization with laboratories in New Mexico, which had already been investigated twice for negligence, including two gruesome deaths.

Roger Fouts, who with his wife, Debbie, has won international acclaim for many years of work in teaching sign language to chimpanzees, says, "When researchers are done with their 'hairy test tubes,' they are usually shattered for the rest of their lives." Something had to be done to save the space chimps.

At that point Carole Noon swept onto the scene. Noon was a former student of Goodall's, whose trip to Africa in the 1980s inspired her to become a wildlife biologist. During a lecture by Goodall at Florida Atlantic University, Noon decided to work with chimps. It was a good fit from the start. She and the chimps enjoyed each other's company. The animals played tricks on her and laughed when she fell for them. They inspired

her admiration for the way they triumphed over the degrada-
tions they had suffered at the hands of humans. Noon had just
finished working in Africa on the project for her doctorate—
mixing chimps orphaned by poachers with foster parent
chimps to form families—when she heard about the space
chimps being turned over to the Coulston Foundation.

Reacting swiftly, Noon petitioned that the chimps be
awarded to the Center for Captive Chimpanzee Care. She was
the founder of the organization but unfortunately as yet had no
facility in which to house the animals. Although she enlisted
Goodall and Fouts to serve on her board of directors and raised
nearly two million dollars, the Air Force still refused to give her
the chimps.

But by securing the backing of thirty-five members of
Congress and the Doris Day Animal League, and with a gift of
one million dollars from the Arcus Foundation, Noon bought
150 acres of a Fort Pierce, Florida, orange grove to build a sanctuary while she sued the Air Force for custody. When she won
custody of twenty-one of the chimps, she moved to a trailer on
her land in order to oversee construction of a home for the Air
Force retirees. The first U.S. sanctuary devoted exclusively to
permanent lifetime care of chimpanzees was begun.

Carole Noon was on her way to providing a secure, en-
riching habitat where the chimps can live a life near to what
their lives would have been had they never been taken from
their homes.

When the space chimps arrived in their new Florida home
in mid-April 2001, Noon expected that some of them would
have psychological problems. However, after being torn from
their mothers, crated and shipped to another continent, spun,
squeezed, bashed, and put in solitary confinement, the chimps
looked around and settled in quietly. They must surely have
felt as though they had been released from a house of horrors.
A second group arrived two months later and, to Noon's
amazement, reacted the same way.

Slowly, the chimps are learning to be chimps again, playing, grooming, brawling, and making up. More chimps will be coming, as they become expendable to researchers or too hard to handle for entertainment. They will form families, but they will not have families. Males will be sterilized. "A sanctuary's goal should be to go out of business solving problems created by someone else," Noon says. The Center for Captive Chimpanzee Care has made an admirable beginning.

A Potpourri of Florida Facts

- Florida became the twenty-seventh state on March 3, 1845.

- Florida has sixty-seven counties. All of Duval County is taken up by the city of Jacksonville, 840 square miles, making Jacksonville one of the largest cities in the U.S.

- Following along her bays and inlets, Florida has 8,400 miles of coastline.

- No point in Florida is more than 60 miles from salt water.

- It is 805 miles from Key West to Pensacola.

- The state's highest elevation is at Lakewood, Florida, 345 feet above sea level. It is lower than the lowest point in sixteen other states.

- Lake Okeechobee, Florida's largest lake, occupies more than 700 square miles.

- Florida has two national parks, Everglades National Park and Biscayne National Park. More than 90% of Biscayne National Park is under water.

- The Apalachicola National Forest covers 557,000 acres.

- Interstate 95, which starts in Maine, passes through sixteen states and ends in downtown Miami.

- The Intracoastal Waterway, which begins in Miami, travels 1,391 miles north to New Jersey.

- The state tree is the sabal palm.

- The state flower is the orange blossom.

- The state beverage is orange juice.

- The state song is "Old Folks at Home," written about Florida's Suwanee River, the name shortened to fit Stephen Foster's melody.

- The state bird is the mockingbird.

- The state animal is the Florida panther.

- The state salt water animal is the dolphin.

- The state fresh water animal is the manatee.

- Florida ranks second only to Hawaii in the number of endangered or threatened species of animals.

- Florida is the largest cattle state east of the Mississippi River.

- Florida mines produce 80% of America's phosphates, 20% of the world's.

- Florida's leading industry is tourism. Agriculture ranks second.

- Ocala leads the state in breeding race horses and is second only to Kentucky in earnings for thoroughbreds.

- Florida grows 79% of the grapefruit and 73% of the oranges sold in the United States. It supplies 80% of the country's orange juice.

- Florida is first in the world as a diving destination.

- Of the cocaine entering America, 70% is believed to pass through Florida.

- Carrabelle, Florida claims the "World's Smallest Police Station." The station is housed in a telephone booth.

- The world's largest scientific building is the Vehicle Assembly Building at Complex 39 at Kennedy Space Center, Cape Canaveral. The building is 716 long, 518 feet wide, and 525 feet long.

- Every February since 1904, Tampa has been captured by "pirates" as part of the Gasparilla Festival, held in memory of pirate José Gaspár.

- The world's longest conga line, at Miami's Calle Ocho festival, made the *Guiness Book of World Records* in 1988 with 119,986 people participating.

- The "Sanibel stoop" is the nonmedical term for the position people assume in bending over sand to pick up shells from one of the best shell-collecting beaches in the world in Sanibel, Florida.

- Possibly the world's most beautiful sunset inspires a round of applause from crowds every day on Mallory Pier in Key West.

- In Lake Wales, Bok Tower's fifty-three bells chime every half-hour. The tower was a gift to his adopted country from Edward Bok, the Dutch-born publisher of *The Ladies Home Journal.*

- The money gathered from the fountains of Walt Disney World is donated to local nonprofit organizations.

- Walt Disney World employs more than 50,000 people in central Florida.

- In the early 1900s, Jacksonville was the center of the filmmaking world that today flourishes in Hollywood, California.

- Florida is home to two major movie facilities, Disney–MGM and Universal Studios, both near Orlando.

- Fort Lauderdale has protected her 6 miles of beach by banning building east of Highway AIA.

- Every year, one out of fifteen Canadians visit Florida. A quarter of a million Canadians live in the state year-round.

- Among those living for a time in Florida are Al Capone, Gloria Estefan, Billy Graham, Wallis Warfield Simpson, Thomas Edison, Marjorie Kinnan Rawlings, Ernest Hemingway, Harriet Beecher Stowe, Henry Ford, Zora Neale Hurston, Ray Charles, Delta Burke, Jackie Gleason, Chris Evert, and the members of singing groups 'NSYNC, the Backstreet Boys, and O-Town.

- At the Daytona International Speedway, the curves are banked so steeply that cars must travel at least 60 miles per hour or risk falling off.

- The frequency of thunderstorms in Florida is higher than any other place in North America.

- Florida Senator Bill Nelson, who underwent intensive training and flew as a crew member on the space shuttle *Columbia,* returned to earth just ten days before *Challenger* lifted off on its doomed flight.

- The most comprehensive collection of art by Louis Comfort Tiffany can be found in Winter Park, Florida.

- President Harry Truman's favorite getaway spot was The Little White House in Key West. While there, he astonished the household help by substituting a shot of bourbon with a chaser of orange juice for the usual cup of coffee every morning. Neither that fact nor his poker table disguised beneath a mahogany cover was ever divulged to the public by the press or household staff.

- Election 2000 wasn't the first time Florida played a pivotal role in the outcome of a presidential election. In 1876, candidate Samuel Tilden needed just one electoral vote to defeat Rutherford Hayes. Louisiana, South Carolina, and Florida were in the undecided column. When Louisiana and South Carolina finally went for Hayes, Florida's four electoral votes, which were decided by less than fifty questionable popular votes, were bartered away in the "Compromise of 1877," a euphemism for the biggest election fix in our history.

Bibliography

General Sources

Gannon, Michael. *Florida, A Short History.* Gainesville, FL: University Press of Florida, 1993.

Kleinberg, Eliot. *Florida Fun Facts.* Sarasota, FL: Pineapple Press, 1995.

Ponce de León's Reception in the New World

Davis, T. Frederick. "History of Juan Ponce de León's Voyages to Florida: Source Records." *Florida Historical Quarterly,* Vol. 14, 1935.

Derr, Mark. *Some Kind of Paradise.* Gainesville, FL: University Press of Florida, 1998.

Fuson, Robert H. *Juan Ponce de León and the Spanish Discovery of Puerto Rico and Florida.* Blacksburg, VA: The McDonald and Woodward Publishing Co., 2000.

Peck, Douglas. *Ponce de León and the Discovery of Florida.* St. Paul, MN: Pogo Press, 1993.

Tebeau, Charlton. *A History of Florida.* Coral Gables, FL: University of Miami Press, 1971.

Osceola Betrayed

Hartley, William & Ellen. *Osceola, The Unconquered Indian.* New York: Hawthorne Books, Inc., 1973.

Seminole Tribune, Hollywood, FL, June 18, 1999.

Ward, May McNeer. "The Disappearance of the Head of Osceola." *Florida Historical Quarterly,* Vol. 33, Nos. 3–4, 1955.

Wickman, Patricia. *Osceola's Legacy.* Tuscaloosa, AL: The University of Alabama Press, 1991.

Dr. Gorrie Makes Ice

Gladstone, John. "Cool It, Said John Gorrie." *South Florida History Magazine,* Spring 1996.

Howe, George D. "The Father of Modern Refrigeration." *Florida Historical Quarterly,* Vol. 1, 1909.

Jahoda, Gloria. *The Other Florida.* New York: Charles Scribner's Sons, 1967.

Barefoot Mailmen

Castello, David J. "The Barefoot Mailman." *The Boyton Beach Times,* Boyton Beach, FL, Oct. 1997.

Oyer, Harvey E., III. "The Barefoot Mailman." *South Florida History,* Vol. 28, No. 4, Fall/Winter 2000.

Pierce, Charles. *Pioneer Life in Southeast Florida.* Coral Gables, FL: University of Miami Press, 1970.

Pratt, Theodore. *The Barefoot Mailman.* Port Salerno, FL: R. Bemis Publishing, Inc., 1993.

A Question of Courage

Peters, Thelma. *Lemon City.* Miami, FL: Banyan Books, Inc., 1976.

Straight, William M., MD. "The Lady Doctor of the Grove." *Journal of the Florida Medical Association,* Vol. 56, No. 8, Aug. 1969.

Henry Flagler's Divorce

Akin, Edward N. *Flagler, Rockefeller Partner and Florida Baron.* Gainesville, FL: University Press of Florida, 1992.

Chandler, David Leon. *Henry Flagler.* New York: Macmillan Publishing Co., 1986.

Martin, Sidney Walter. *Florida's Flagler.* Athens, GA: University of Georgia Press, 1949.

Tampa Nurse Builds a Hospital

Adams, John Henry. "The Clara Frye Hospital." *The Negro Blue Book of Tampa,* circa 1925.

Brady, Rowena. *Things Remembered, An Album of African Americans in Tampa.* Tampa, FL: University of Tampa Press, 1997.

Colburn, David R. and Jane L. Landers, eds. *The African American Heritage of Florida.* Gainesville, FL: University Press of Florida, 1995.

Tampa Morning Tribune, Tampa, FL, April 9, 1936.

The Tampa Tribune-Times, Tampa, FL, Feb. 26, 1989.

The Tampa Tribune, Tampa, FL, July 8, 1990.

A Chinese Man's Faith in America

Furnas, J. C. *The Americans.* New York: G. P. Putnam's Sons, 1969.

McCunn, Ruthanne L. *Chinese American Portraits.* San Francisco, CA: Chronicle Books, 1988.

Murry, Marian. *Plant Wizard, The Life of Lue Gim Gong.* New York: Macmillan Co., 1970.

Press Journal, Vero Beach, FL, May 13, 2001.

Weaver, Brian and Richard. *The Citrus Industry.* Charleston, SC: Arcadia Publishing, 1999.

Flying on Schedule

Arsenault, Raymond. *St. Petersburg and the American Dream.* Gainesville, FL: University Press of Florida, 1996.

Glines, C. V. "World's First Winged Airline," *Aviation History,* June 1997.

Reilly, Thomas. *Jannus, An American Flier.* Gainesville, FL: University Press of Florida, 1997.

———. "The St. Petersburg-Tampa Airboat Line: 90 Days that Changed the World of Aviation." *Tampa Bay History,* Vol. 18, No. 2, Fall/Winter 1996.

Carl and His Elephant

Foster, Mark S. *Castles in the Sand.* Gainesville, FL: University Press of Florida, 2000.

Redford, Polly. *Billion-Dollar Sandbar.* New York: E. P. Dutton & Company, Inc., 1970.

Marjory's Poem

Carper, N. Gordon. "Martin Tabert, Martyr of an Era." *Florida Historical Quarterly,* Vol. 52, 1973.

Douglas, Marjory Stoneman. *Voice of the River.* Sarasota, FL: Pineapple Press, 1987.

Eckert, Edward. "Contract Labor in Florida During Reconstruction." *Florida Historical Quarterly,* No. 47, 1968.

Powell, J. C. *The American Siberia*. Gainesville, FL: University Press of Florida, 1976.

Saving Betty Mae

Jahoda, Gloria. *Florida, A Bicentennial History*. New York: W. W. Norton & Co., 1976.

Jumper, Betty Mae. *Legends of the Seminoles*. Sarasota, FL: Pineapple Press, 1994.

McCarthy, Kevin. *Native Americans in Florida*. Sarasota, FL: Pineapple Press, 1999.

The Seminole Tribune, Vol. XX, No. 29, September 11, 1998.

Nazis Invade Florida

Farrant, Don. "Up Periscope." *Florida Living Magazine,* Feb. 1999.

Forum, The Magazine of the Florida Humanities Council, Vol. XXII, No. 3, 1999.

Huckshorn, Robert J. *Government and Politics in Florida.* Gainesville, FL: University Press of Florida, 1991.

Kleinberg, Eliot. *War in Paradise*. Melbourne, FL: The Florida Historical Society Press, 1999.

Prior, Leon O. "Nazi Invasion of Florida." *Florida Historical Quarterly,* Vol. 49, No. 2, Oct. 1970.

A Small Patch of Cuba

Greenbaum, Susan D. *Afro-Cubans in Ybor City*. Tampa, FL: University of South Florida, 1986.

Harner, Charles E. *A Pictorial History of Ybor City*. Tampa, FL: Trend Publications, Inc., 1975.

Hewitt, Nancy A. "Varieties of Voluntarism: Class, Ethnicity, and Women's Activism in Tampa." *Women, Politics and Change.* New York: Russell Sage Foundation, 1990.

Mormino, Gary and Anthony Pizzo. *Tampa, The Treasure City.* Tulsa, OK: Continental Heritage Press, 1983.

Poyo, Gerald E. "A Woman's Place in Building a Grass Roots Victory." *Forum.* Vol. 18, No. 2, Summer 1995.

de Qesada, A. M. *Images of America.* Charleston, SC: Arcadia Publishing, 1999.

Cuban Missile Crisis

Florida Times-Union, Jacksonville, FL, Oct. 4, 1997, Jan. 20, 2001, Jan. 21, 2001.

Kennedy, Robert F. *Thirteen Days.* New York: W. W. Norton & Company, 1969.

National Security Archives, Washington, D.C., Aug. 2, 2001, Aug. 30, 2001.

Orlando Sentinel, Orlando, FL, Jan. 12, 2001.

Time, Vol. LXXX, No. 18, Nov. 2, 1962.

Philanthropist Solves a Mystery

Graymont, Barbara. *The MacArthur Heritage, The Story of an American Family.* Chicago, IL: The John D. and Catherine T. MacArthur Foundation, 1993.

Hoffman, William. *The Stockholder.* New York: Lyle Stuart, Inc., 1969.

Nash, Jay Robert. *Jack Murphy, Encyclopedia of World Crime.* Wilmette, IL: Crime Books, Inc., 1990.

Newsweek, Nov. 16, 1964, Vol. LXIV, No. 20.

Sanford, Bob. *John D. MacArthur: A View From the Bar.* Highland City, FL: Rainbow Books, Inc., 1996.

Time, Jan. 15, 1965, Vol. 85, No. 3.

Time, Sept. 10, 1965, Vol. 86, No. 1.

Dr. Cade Wins the Orange Bowl

"Father of Gatorade and Wife Fund Professorship," *Florida Physician,* Fall 1999.

"Fifty People Who Made a Difference: Robert Cade," *Gainesville Sun,* July 6, 2001.

University of Florida Oral History Program, Transcript of interview with Dr. Cade. Received Dec. 13, 2000.

Tired Housewife from Micanopy

Audubon News, Florida Audubon Society, Oct. 10, 1997.

Carr, Marjorie Harris. "A Florida Scandal." Florida Defenders of the Environment, Nov. 1996.

Derr, Mark. *Some Kind of Paradise.* Gainesville, FL: University Press of Florida, 1998.

"Fifty People Who Made a Difference: Marjorie Carr," *Gainesville Sun,* Oct. 8, 2000.

Ocklawaha River Restoration, History of Restoration Efforts. Florida Defenders of the Environment, Nov. 28, 2000.

The Monitor, Vol. 18, No. 3, Winter 1999 and Vol. 19, No. 3, Fall 2000.

How the Mouse Got His Kingdom

"Empire of the Sun." *U.S. News & World Report.* May 28, 1990, Vol. 108, No. 21.

Fogelsong, Richard E. *Married to the Mouse*. New Haven, CT: Yale University Press, 2001.

Frearson, Steve. *A History of the Walt Disney World Resort*. Burbank, CA: 2000.

Orlando Sentinel, Orlando, FL, Dec. 16, 2001, Dec. 17, 2001, Dec. 18, 2001, Dec. 19, 2001.

Walt Disney World. Walt Disney Productions, 1981.

The Last Straw

Florida State Archives, Roxcy Bolton Collection, Series 1394, Carton 22 and Series M94-1, Carton 2.

Miami Herald, Miami, FL, Feb. 28, 1984, Oct. 18, 1988, Nov. 9, 1990, May 9, 1994, Dec. 10, 1998, Aug. 27, 1999.

The New York Times, New York, NY, Sept. 11, 2000.

Give Kids the World

Landwirth, Henri. *Gift of Life*. Privately published, circa 1996.

Los Angeles Times, Oct. 15, 2000.

Lowe, Cindy. "Give Kids The World!" *Florida Living Magazine,* Oct. 1988.

Travis McGee Day

MacDonald, John D. *Bright Orange for the Shroud*. New York: Fawcett Crest, 1965.

———. *Darker Than Amber*. New York: Fawcett Crest, 1966.

———. *The Deep Blue Good-by*. New York: Fawcett Crest, 1964.

Merrill, Hugh. *The Red Hot Typewriter*. New York: St. Martin's Press, 2000.

A Granny Goes on Trial

Bovard, Wendy and Gladys Milton. *Why Not Me?* Summerton, TN: The Book Publishing Company, 1993.

DeFuniak Herald, DeFuniak, FL, June 24, 1999.

Griffin, Katherine. "Gladys." *Health Magazine,* May/June 1992.

National Center for Health Statistics, Press Release, May 19, 1998.

Susie, Debra Anne. *In the Way of Our Grandmothers.* Athens, GA: University of Georgia Press, 1988.

USA Today, Nov. 10, 1995.

Art Deco Queen Fights City Hall

Capitman, Barbara Baer. *Deco Delights.* New York: E. P. Dutton, 1988.

———. & Michael Kinerk & Dennis W. Wilhelm. *Rediscovering Art Deco USA.* New York: Viking Studio Books, 1994.

Miami Herald, Apr. 1, 1990.

New York Times, Feb. 7, 1988.

O'Connor, Lona. "The Queen of Art Deco Fights On." *Historic Preservation,* Sept./Oct. 1989.

Wisser, Bill. *South Beach.* New York: Arcade Publishing, 1995.

Driving Miss Diamond

Memorial program, *Dedication of The Diamond Family Social Hall,* Feb. 22, 1985.

Photocopies from The Ruby Diamond Collection at Florida State University Library, Tallahassee, FL, June 1, 1967.

Tallahassee Democrat, March 11, 1990.

Transcripts of interview with Ruby Diamond, Florida State Archives, Apr. 18, 1970.

Andrew Blows Into Town

Kleinberg, Howard. *The Florida Hurricane & Disaster 1992.* Miami, FL: Centennial Press, 1992.

Miami Herald Staff. *The Big One, Hurricane Andrew.* Miami, FL: The Miami Herald Publishing Co., 1992.

Moore, Marilyn A. "After the Big One." *South Florida Magazine,* Vol. 45, No. 12, Oct. 1992.

Staff of Sun-Sentinel, Fort Lauderdale, FL. *Andrew!* Orlando, FL: Tribune Publishing, 1992.

Right Stuff, Wrong Gender

America's Sports Car, Bowling Green, KY: National Corvette Museum, June 3, 2001.

Cooper, Ann. "Betty Skelton: An Exceptional Woman." *Woman Pilot Magazine,* September/October 1998.

Correspondence from Betty Skelton Frankman to author, June 12, 2001.

Florida Today, June 21, 1998.

Holden, Henry M. "Women in Space—The Mercury 13." *World Airnews,* August 1999.

Look, Vol. 24, No. 3, Feb. 2, 1960.

Steadman, Bernice Trimble. *Tethered Mercury.* Traverse City, MI: Aviation Press, 2001.

Butterflies and Ballots

Correspondents of *The New York Times. 36 Days.* New York: Times Books, Henry Holt & Co., 2001.

Gleick, J. *Chaos.* New York: Penguin Books, 1997.

Linder, Doug. "Of Ballots and Butterfly Wings." University of Missouri-Kansas Law School, Nov. 15, 2000.

Staff of *The Miami Herald. The Miami Herald Report.* New York: St. Martin's Press, 2001.

Staff of the *Washington Post. Deadlock.* New York: Public Affairs, 2001.

Space Chimps Retire

Center for Captive Chimpanzee Care Newsletter, Vol. 1, Issue 1, Fall 2000.

Fort Lauderdale Sun-Sentinel, Jan. 31, 2001.

Fort Pierce Tribune, Feb. 9, 2001.

Las Vegas Review Journal, Aug. 7, 1998.

Orlando Sentinel, July 31, 2001.

Palm Beach Post, March 15, 2001.

Index

About the Author

A Pennsylvanian now residing in Vero Beach, Florida, a lover of books and history, E. Lynne Wright was a nurse anesthetist, wife, and mother of three before embarking on a writing career. Since then, her short stories, nonfiction articles, essays, and book reviews have appeared in the *Cleveland Plain Dealer, Hartford Courant, Mature Lifestyles, Woman's Day,* and numerous anthologies and literary magazines. Exploring Florida by land and boat has inspired a love for the state's natural beauty, its people, and its history. Lynne is also the author of *More than Petticoats: Remarkable Florida Women.*